15 Days of Prayer
With Saint Teresa of Ávila

Also in the *15 Days of Prayer* collection:

15 DAYS OF PRAYER
WITH
Saint Teresa of Ávila

JEAN ABIVEN

Translated by Victoria Hébert and Denis Sabourin

Liguori
LIGUORI, MISSOURI

Published by Liguori Publications
Liguori, Missouri
http://www.liguori.org

This book is a translation of *Prier 15 Jours Avec Saint Thérèse d'Avila,* published by Nouvelle Cité, 1993, Montrouge, France.

Library of Congress Cataloging-in-Publication Data

Jean Abiven
    [Prier 15 jours avec Saint Thérèse d'Ávila. English]
    15 days of prayer with Saint Teresa of Ávila / Jean Abiven ; [translated by] Victoria Hébert and Denis Sabourin. — 1st English ed.
        p.   cm.
    Includes bibliographical references.
    ISBN 0-7648-0573-8 (pbk)
    1. Teresa, of Avila, Saint, 1515–1582—Meditations. 2. Spiritual life—Catholic Church. I. Title: Fifteen days of prayer with Saint Teresa of Avila. II. Title.

BX4700.T4 A4213 2000
269'6—dc21   99–055492

Printed in the United States of America
04 03 02 01 00   5 4 3 2 1
First English Edition 2000

Table of Contents

How to Use This Book

AN OLD CHINESE PROVERB, or at least what I am able to recall of what is supposed to be an old Chinese proverb, goes something like this: "Even a journey of a thousand miles begins with a single step." When you think about it, the truth of the proverb is obvious. It is impossible to begin any project, let alone a journey, without taking the first step. I think it might also be true, although I cannot recall if another Chinese proverb says it, "that the first step is often the hardest." Or, as someone else once observed, "the distance between a thought and the corresponding action needed to implement the idea takes the most energy." I don't know who shared that perception with me but I am certain it was not an old Chinese master!

With this ancient proverbial wisdom, and the not-so-ancient wisdom of an unknown contemporary sage still fresh, we move from proverbs to presumptions. How do these relate to the task before us?

I am presuming that if you are reading this introduction it is because you are contemplating a journey. My presumption is that you are preparing for a spiritual journey and that you have taken at least some of the first steps necessary to prepare for this journey. I also presume, and please excuse me if I am making too many presumptions, that in your preparation for the spiritual journey you have determined that you need a guide.

From deep within the recesses of your deepest self, there was something that called you to consider Saint Teresa as a potential companion. If my presumptions are correct, may I congratulate you on this decision? I think you have made a wise choice, a choice that can be confirmed by yet another source of wisdom, the wisdom that comes from practical experience.

Even an informal poll of experienced travelers will reveal a common opinion; it is very difficult to travel alone. Some might observe that it is even foolish. Still others may be even stronger in their opinion and go so far as to insist that it is necessary to have a guide, especially when you are traveling into uncharted waters and into territory that you have not yet experienced. I am of the personal opinion that a traveling companion is welcome under all circumstances. The thought of traveling alone, to some exciting destination without someone to share the journey with does not capture my imagination or channel my enthusiasm. However, with that being noted, what is simply a matter of preference on the normal journey becomes a matter of necessity when a person embarks on a spiritual journey.

The spiritual journey, which can be the most challenging of all journeys, is experienced best with a guide, a companion, or at the very least, a friend in whom you have placed your trust. This observation is not a preference or an opinion but rather an established spiritual necessity. All of the great saints with whom I am familiar had a spiritual director or a confessor who journeyed with them. Admittedly, at times the saint might well have traveled far beyond the experience of their guide and companion but more often than not they would return to their director and reflect on their experience. Understood in this sense, the director and companion provided a valuable contribution and necessary resource.

When I was learning how to pray (a necessity for anyone who desires to be a full-time and public "religious person"), the community of men that I belong to gave me a great gift. Between my second and third year in college, I was given a one-year sabbatical, with all expenses paid and all of my personal needs met. This period of time was called novitiate. I was officially designated as a novice, a beginner in the spiritual journey, and I was assigned a "master," a person who was willing to lead me. In addition to the master, I was provided with every imaginable book and any other resource that I could possibly need. Even with all that I was provided, I did not learn how to pray because of the books and the unlimited resources, rather it was the master, the companion who was the key to the experience.

One day, after about three months of reading, of quiet and solitude, and of practicing all of the methods and descriptions of prayer that were available to me, the master called. "Put away the books, forget the method, and just listen." We went into a room, became quiet, and tried to recall the presence of God, and then, the master simply prayed out loud and permitted me to listen to his prayer. As he prayed, he revealed his hopes, his dreams, his struggles, his successes, and most of all, his relationship with God. I discovered as I listened that his prayer was deeply intimate but most of all it was self-revealing. As I learned about him, I was led through his life experience to the place where God dwells. At that moment I was able to understand a little bit about what I was supposed to do if I really wanted to pray.

The dynamic of what happened when the master called, invited me to listen, and then revealed his innermost self to me as he communicated with God in prayer, was important. It wasn't so much that the master was trying to reveal to me what needed to be said; he was not inviting me to pray with the same words that he used, but rather that he was trying to bring me to that place within myself where prayer becomes possible. That place, a place of intimacy and of self-awareness, was a necessary stop on the journey and it was a place that I needed to be led to. I could not have easily discovered it on my own.

The purpose of the volume that you hold in your hand is to lead you, over a period of fifteen days or, maybe more realistically, fifteen prayer periods, to a place where prayer is possible. If you already have a regular experience and practice of prayer, perhaps this volume can help lead you to a deeper place, a more intimate relationship with the Lord.

It is important to note that the purpose of this book is not to lead you to a better relationship with Saint Teresa, your spiritual companion. Although your companion will invite you to share some of their deepest and most intimate thoughts, your companion is doing so only to bring you to that place where God dwells. After all, the true measurement of a companion for the journey is that they bring you to the place where you need to be, and then they step back, out of the picture. A guide who brings you to the desired destination and then sticks around is a very unwelcome guest!

Many times I have found myself attracted to a particular idea or method for accomplishing a task, only to discover that what seemed to be inviting and helpful possessed too many details. All of my energy went to the mastery of the details and I soon lost my enthusiasm. In each instance, the book that seemed so promising ended up on my bookshelf, gathering dust. I can assure you, it is not our intention that this book end up in your bookcase, filled with promise, but unable to deliver.

There are three simple rules that need to be followed in order to use this book with a measure of satisfaction.

Place: It is important that you choose a place for reading that provides the necessary atmosphere for reflection and that does not allow for too many distractions. Whatever place you choose needs to be comfortable, have the necessary lighting, and, finally, have a sense of "welcoming" about it. You need to be able to look forward to the experience of the journey. Don't travel steerage if you know you will be more comfortable in first class and if the choice is realistic for you. On the other hand, if first class is a distraction and you feel more comfortable and more yourself in steerage, then it is in steerage that you belong.

My favorite place is an overstuffed and comfortable chair in my bedroom. There is a light over my shoulder, and the chair reclines if I feel a need to recline. Once in a while, I get lucky and the sun comes through my window and bathes the entire room in light. I have other options and other places that are available to me but this is the place that I prefer.

Time: Choose a time during the day when you are most alert and when you are most receptive to reflection, meditation, and prayer. The time that you choose is an essential component. If you are a morning person, for example, you should choose a time that is in the morning. If you are more alert in the afternoon, choose an afternoon time slot; and if evening is your preference, then by all means choose the evening. Try to avoid "peak" periods in your daily routine when you know that you might be disturbed. The time that you choose needs to be your time and needs to work for you.

It is also important that you choose how much time you

will spend with your companion each day. For some it will be possible to set aside enough time in order to read and reflect on all the material that is offered for a given day. For others, it might not be possible to devote one time to the suggested material for the day, so the prayer period may need to be extended for two, three, or even more sessions. It is not important how long it takes you; it is only important that it works for you and that you remain committed to that which is possible.

For myself I have found that fifteen minutes in the early morning, while I am still in my robe and pajamas and before my morning coffee, and even before I prepare myself for the day, is the best time. No one expects to see me or to interact with me because I have not yet "announced" the fact that I am awake or even on the move. However, once someone hears me in the bathroom, then my window of opportunity is gone. It is therefore important to me that I use the time that I have identified when it is available to me.

Freedom: It may seem strange to suggest that freedom is the third necessary ingredient, but I have discovered that it is most important. By freedom I understand a certain "stance toward life," a "permission to be myself and to be gentle and understanding of who I am." I am constantly amazed at how the human person so easily sets himself or herself up for disappointment and perceived failure. We so easily make judgments about ourselves and our actions and our choices, and very often those judgments are negative, and not at all helpful.

For instance, what does it really matter if I have chosen a place and a time, and I have missed both the place and the time for three days in a row? What does it matter if I have chosen, in that twilight time before I am completely awake and still a little sleepy, to roll over and to sleep for fifteen minutes more? Does it mean that I am not serious about the journey, that I really don't want to pray, that I am just fooling myself when I say that my prayer time is important to me? Perhaps, but I prefer to believe that it simply means that I am tired and I just wanted a little more sleep. It doesn't mean anything more than that. However, if I make it mean more than that, then I can become discouraged, frustrated, and put myself into a state where I might more easily give up. "What's the use? I might as well forget all about it."

The same sense of freedom applies to the reading and the praying of this text. If I do not find the introduction to each day helpful, I don't need to read it. If I find the questions for reflection at the end of the appointed day repetitive, then I should choose to close the book and go my own way. Even if I discover that the reflection offered for the day is not the one that I prefer and that the one for the next day seems more inviting, then by all means, go on to the one for the next day.

That's it! If you apply these simple rules to your journey you should receive the maximum benefit and you will soon find yourself at your destination. But be prepared to be surprised. If you have never been on a spiritual journey you should know that the "travel brochures" and the other descriptions that you might have heard are nothing compared to the real thing. There is so much more than you can imagine.

A final prayer of blessing suggests itself:

> Lord, catch me off guard today.
> Surprise me with some moment of beauty
>   or pain
> So that at least for the moment
> I may be startled into seeing that you are
>   here in all your splendor,
> Always and everywhere,
> Barely hidden,
> Beneath,
> Beyond,
> Within this life I breathe.

Frederick Buechner

REV. THOMAS M. SANTA, CSsR
LIGUORI, MISSOURI
FEAST OF THE PRESENTATION, 1999

A Brief Chronology of Saint Teresa's Life

THE YEAR WAS 1515; it was an era of change they called the Renaissance. America had recently been discovered. "The earth is round!" It revolved around the sun, even if it appeared that the holiest of books, the Bible, seemed to confirm the opposite. What were people to believe? The old and sacred certainties were less certain. It was a time when many things were doubted, questioned, researched, and discovered. And in the midst of it all, human beings suddenly became aware of their interiority, and this renewed experience of the world drew them to become the masters of wisdom.

It was into such a world that Teresa of Ávila was born—Teresa: a mystic, a religious reformer, the foundress of seventeen convents, the author of four books, and one of the great masters of Christian prayer. She was a woman who would not only leave her mark in her native country, but also on the religious world by becoming the first woman to be raised to the level of Doctor of the Catholic Church. The following is a shortened chronology of her celebrated life.

1515: Teresa Sanchez Cepeda Davila y Ahumada was born on March 28 in Ávila, Old Castile, Spain; the third child (of ten) of Don Alonso Sanchez de Cepeda and Dona Beatriz Davila y Ahumada (who became Don Alonzo's second wife at the age of fifteen, after his first wife and the mother of two of his children died).

—Teresa was of the nobility from her mother's family; her father, a merchant and saintly man, was the son of a forcibly converted Jew.

1522–1529:

—At the age of seven, Teresa attempted to run away from home with her beloved brother Rodrigo, spurred on by visions of being beheaded at the hands of the Moors in the name of Christ.

—Her piety waned somewhat, and she became interested in chivalry. Teresa became particularly attracted to her cousins—a fact that her father disliked greatly.

—In 1529, Teresa's mother died, throwing Teresa into a state of acute loneliness; she appealed to the Blessed Virgin Mary to become her mother.

1530–1534:

—Seeing her need for guidance in 1531, her father sent her to school (Our Lady of Grace) with the Augustinian sisters close by where, under the influence of the school mistress, Teresa was able to regain her sense of piety.

—In 1532, she left school due to illness, spending time recovering at her uncle's home, where she became acquainted with the letters of Saint Jerome—these made her determined to adopt the religious life—not so much due to a firm conviction for, or attraction to it, but as a means of taking "the safest course." Her father was greatly opposed to her decision, and she was unable to obtain his consent to enter the convent.

1535–1553:

—Teresa left home and, on November 2, 1535, entered the Carmelite convent of the Incarnation at Ávila; her father finally gave his consent, and she professed her vows the following year.

—Shortly after her profession in 1536, she became seriously ill; many cures were sought, both conventional and folk; she was forced to return home in 1539.

—In August of 1539, she fell into a coma that was so profound that she was thought to have died—but four days later she regained consciousness, though her legs remained paralyzed for the next three years. She attributed her partial cure to the intercession of Saint Joseph; but after these events, her health would remain permanently impaired.

—This was a dark period for Teresa: a period of mediocrity in her spiritual life; she never gave up on prayer (although some sources report her as giving up on it for a period of three years). This period of darkness would last some eighteen years, during which time she had transitory mystical experiences.

—In 1543, Teresa returned home to care for her dying father and assisted him until his death in December.

1554–1559:

—At the age of thirty-nine, she began to enjoy a vivid experience of God's presence within her; she experienced a profound conversion before the statue of the wounded Christ.

—These were years of conflict for Teresa; many thought that her visions were the devil's work, and even some of her confessors tried to convince her of this.

—In 1555, Francis Borgia heard her confession and told her that God's spirit was working in her and that she should concentrate on Christ's passion and not resist the ecstatic experiences that came to her in prayer. The divine favors increased in spite of the distrust of her friends; and she began to identify herself with two penitents, Mary Magdalene and Saint Augustine.

—In 1559, the intellectual visions of Christ began.

1560–1561:

—In 1560, Teresa began having visions of the risen Christ and received the grace of transverberation, the piercing of the heart in a heavenly vision; she also had her frightening vision of hell.

—Discussions about a new foundation begin as a result of Teresa's unhappiness with unreformed Carmelite life; she wanted to found a house where the rule would be strictly observed. There was much opposition to this.

—One September evening in 1560, a group met in her cell, proposing to found an eremetical monastery based on the primitive tradition of Carmel and the discalced reform of Saint Peter of Alcantara (note: discalced literally means "shoeless," yet the sisters did wear hemp sandals, but the name referred to the strict poverty that would be a feature of her reform; the religious would live entirely by alms and their own labor; they would be vegetarians and adhere to a rigorous schedule of prayer).

—Teresa began her first draft for her book, *Life*....

—In 1561, Saint Clare promised to help Teresa as Teresa performed her first miracle—bringing her nephew back to life.

1562–1567:

—February 7, 1562, saw Teresa receiving an apostolic rescript allowing her to make the new foundation she so desired.

—She finished her book, *Life*....

—The foundation of the new monastery of Saint Joseph (August 24, 1562) is laid; four novices received the habit of the

Discalced Carmelites. Legal battles ensued but they were resolved by the end of that year.

—In 1563, Teresa was named prioress of Saint Joseph and wrote her *Constitutions*.

—In 1566, she wrote *The Way of Perfection* and her *Meditations on the Song of Songs*.

1567–1571:

—In 1567, she received authorization to found other monasteries; she met Saint John of the Cross and convinced him to join her in her work.

—Her foundations included the following: Medina del Campo (1567); Malagon and Valladolid (1568); Toledo and Pastrana (1569); Salamanca (1570); Alba (1571); as well as two for Discalced Friars: Duruelo (1568) and Pastrana (1569).

—She was asked and reluctantly agreed to become prioress at the Incarnation.

1572–1577:

—On November 18, 1572, while receiving communion from Saint John of the Cross (now chaplain), she received the grace of the "spiritual marriage."

—In 1573, she began to write her book, *Foundations*.

—A second series of foundations began: Segovia (1574); Beas and Seville (1575); Caravaca (1576).

—In 1575, she was denounced to the Inquisition at Seville and ordered by her chapter to retire to one of her monasteries in Castile.

—In 1576, she answered the Inquisition and wrote *On Making the Visitation*.

—During the period June to November, 1577, she wrote *The Interior Castle*; in early December, Saint John of the Cross is arrested; Teresa wrote to the king on his behalf, unfortunately with little effect.

—Teresa fell down a flight of stairs on December 24 and broke her left arm—it was not set properly and she is left permanently incapacitated.

1578–1579:

—Saint John of the Cross escaped from prison in 1578 (August).

—There was great conflict between the Calced and Discalced; they were separated and a Discalced province was established.

—A new monastery to her strict specifications (the only one) was built in Malagon; the nuns moved into it.

1580–1581:

—Teresa returned to visiting her convents and resumed her foundations: Villaneuva (1580); and Palencia and Soria (1581).

1582: Teresa left Ávila for the last time on her way to the new foundation at Burgos; Granada was founded by Saint John of the Cross and the Venerable Anne of Jesus, as Teresa was too ill to assist; she left for Alba.

—September 29, she took to her bed, seriously ill, announcing that her death was near.

—October 3, Teresa received the sacrament of reconciliation and of the sick.

—October 4, she died at 9:00 P.M., at the age of sixty-seven.

—The Gregorian Calendar was introduced that year, so the day following Teresa's death became October 15.

Teresa's body was buried in Alba after her death; after some years, it was returned to Ávila, but later reconveyed to Alba, where it is still preserved incorrupt. Her heart clearly shows the marks of the transverberation.

Teresa was beatified by Pope Paul V on April 24, 1614; she was proclaimed the Patroness of Spain in 1615; Pope Gregory XV canonized her on March 12, 1622, fixing her feast day as October 15. On September 27, 1970, she was declared a Doctor of the Church by Pope Paul VI, becoming the first woman saint to be recognized as such. Her usual emblems are a fiery arrow or a dove above her head.

Saint Teresa's written works hold a unique position among mystical writers. Her writings are about her own experiences which her profound insight and analytical graces enable her to clearly explain. Her writings are extremely personal, extending themselves to the limitations imposed by her own experiences but no further.

Introduction

YOU ARE GOING TO SPEND fifteen days, dear reader friend, in the company of Teresa of Ávila; or, more precisely, you will spend fifteen days in the company of the Lord with Teresa's help. Perhaps it was her precious name that attracted you to this book. Perhaps it was the simple desire to spend a period of spiritual respiration, retreat, or uplift with respect to your daily life. No matter what the reason! In all cases, these fifteen days presuppose a path to follow, and the initial pages will tell you where you will be going, just as an itinerary on a map. You will discover the landscape by making the journey.

Saint Ignatius of Loyola, in his *Exercises*, proposed a methodology to his retreatants which takes them, step by step, to a discernment of what the Lord wants from them within the concrete conditions of the time and environment in which they live. And, by doing this, Ignatius prompts them to successively adopt new attitudes—attitudes which are the hallmarks of human beings when they are faced with God. The procedure employed in his *Exercises* has no other equivalent in any other spiritual tradition; from that point on, this method became a part of the common treasure of the Church.

This book does not pretend to propose following the method of Saint Ignatius' *Exercises*, assisted instead by

Teresa's texts. That would be risky and, in the best event, the result would be only an artificial replica. But we do not have to forget the Ignatian method in order to travel this road with our saint. As much this one as the other, as long as it doesn't impose a yoke on Teresa's message that would betray it. However, Teresa has nothing other to tell us than what has happened to her. And, in her writings, we will find the progression of a soul which, at a young age, asks itself fundamental questions, battles against sin, gives itself to Christ with all of its spark, a soul which must continue to discern how to reach him in her daily life and how to recognize him through the favors she has been granted. Indeed, the actions of her whole life serve as witnesses to a constant prayerful union with the Lord. Thus, dear reader, do not be surprised to discover at some points a familiar road that you already may know if you have followed the *Exercises*.

Here then are the stages we are proposing for this journey with Saint Teresa. Some stages on the journey are two or three days long, depending on the case, which will permit you to stop and take a break if you have the need to do so.

1. Days 1 and 2: Getting onto the road; how do we pray?; Who am I in the eyes of God?
2. Days 3 and 4: The merciful benevolence of the Savior to the sinner that I am.
3. Days 5, 6, and 7: Jesus presents himself to me, asking, "Do you want to follow me?"
4. Days 8 and 9: What do I do, Lord, to join you?
5. Days 10, 11, and 12: Discerning the Lord's initiatives.
6. Days 13, 14, and 15: Remaining united to him in our daily lives through service to the Church.

The titles for each day are borrowed from Teresa's own writings. They could make up what we used to call a "spiritual banquet": a sort of summary or prospectus to mull over during the passage of each day's journey. The texts themselves are extracted from the saint's writings, which are, at times, arranged into groupings made up of passages from different works. References are given for each, so if you feel that you want to investigate one or more passages in depth, you may easily do so. The bibliography at the end of the book will also assist you in your search for additional information and inspiration.

Abbreviations Used in This Book

V   The Collected Works of Saint Teresa of Ávila (*The Life...*)

C   *The Way of Perfection*

D   *The Interior Castle* (divided into seven dwelling places which are noted from 1D to 7D)

E   Exclamations

F   The Foundations

P   Thoughts about the Love of God

Po Poetry by Saint Teresa of Ávila

FVD Favors Granted by God

R   The Letters of Saint Teresa of Jesus

DAY ONE

The Business of Friendship

Every moment we spend in the presence of a friend is precious. It does not matter how that time is spent. Watching a movie, fishing, eating dinner, or having a heart-to-heart conversation—the joy of friendship is the *time* spent in the other's company. The same is true of prayer. Prayer needn't be my continual effort to "make conversation." Surely, my friendship with God is not dependent on that! The joy of friendship with God in prayer is the *time* spent in prayer with God. This can be quiet time (wordless contemplation), serious, heart-to-heart time, playful talking, or simply listening.

*Mental prayer, in my opinion, is nothing other than an inti-
mate sharing between friends; it means taking time frequently
to be alone with the One who we know loves us (V, 8/5).*

*Then, daughters, since you are alone, strive to find a compan-
ion. Well, what better companion [could you have] than the
Master himself who taught you this prayer? Picture the Lord
himself as close to you and behold how lovingly and humbly
he is teaching you. Believe me, you should remain with so good
a friend as long as you can. If you grow accustomed to him
present at your side, and he sees that you do so with love and
that you go about striving to please him, you will not be able—
as they say—to get away from him; he will never fail you; he
will help you in all your trials; you will find him everywhere
(C, 26/1).*

*Now, I'm not asking you to think about him or to draw out a
lot of concepts or make long and subtle reflections with your
intellect. I'm not asking you to do anything more than look at
him (C, 26/3).*

*They say that for a woman to be a good wife toward her hus-
band she must be sad when he is sad, and joyful when he is
joyful, even though she may not be so. (See what subjection
you have been freed from, Sisters!) The Lord, without decep-
tion, truly acts in such a way with us. He is the one who submits, and he wants you to be the lady with authority to rule;
he submits to your will. If you are joyful, look at him as risen
(...). If you are experiencing trials or are sad, behold him on
the way to the garden [of Olives] (...). Or behold him bound
to the column, filled with pain, with all his flesh torn in pieces
for the great love he bears you (C, 26/4–5).*

These passages set the tone for the beginning of your encounters with Teresa. As one would have suspected, Teresa, admirably gifted to keep company or hold a conversation, does not imagine a relationship with God to be anything other than this. She invites us to take part in "the business of friendship." She thus parallels the attitude of the prophet Elijah, who is the Father of the Carmelites: "The God before me who I hold close to me is alive" (1 R 17, 1).

Lord, in order to pray, there must be two of us. Since you are always there, all we have to do is establish ourselves in your presence and dwell there. Everything is there. Without a doubt, for Teresa, as for each of us, the problem will be what to do once we are in the presence of God. But everything must follow in its own time. First, what is essential is to be there, to be there with God in friendship.

What that means is that in prayer "it is not necessary to think too much, but to love a great deal." Teresa repeated this formula many times. Two older spouses, who are very united and know each other intimately, could have a heart-to-heart conversation without uttering many words. An intense current of affection circulates between them. It is like this when you meet the Lord in prayer. Certainly, distractions may occur: we can't stop our imaginations from wandering. Simply, when we perceive them, we must return to what we were doing and come back to the Lord, to his presence. Some people may well spontaneously return to the subject of their prayer. This spontaneous return from distraction may be a valuable strategy. But this does not represent Teresa's attitude. All of those who find themselves to be like her will first need to come back, as she did, to the company of God.

In this friendship relationship, the Lord is the principal speaker. We always think that it is up to us to act, for us to make conversation. We believe that its success depends solely upon us! And we deserve this gentle reproach that Jesus made to Martha: "You get too excited over too many things!" or one made to a Carmelite: "Could you let me get a word in edgewise?" We must ask the Lord to teach us to allow ourselves to "establish ourselves in him, immobile and quiet, as if our soul is already in eternity." Elizabeth of the Trinity, who wrote this request, is truly a daughter of Teresa of Jesus. You, Lord, are the one who has something to say to us. You already speak to us through your very silence, which soothes our agitations, and which compels us to endure through faith.

It could also happen that you speak to us through a certain verse of Scripture, which had been read and reread, but today, we see it as if we have read it for the very first time, with a bounty of meaning, as if it has been expressly said for us. And even if this rarely happens—for it happens only when the reader wants it to—our faithfulness in coming to the meeting with the Lord, coming into your presence, results in shaping us in your image. Lord, just as elderly mothers of priests, whose long lives of prayer and humble denial result in a "knowledge" of you, all knowing, indescribable, and sometimes more profound than that of their sons who are graduates of schools of theology. Lord, you are a sun—a sun created so that it shines and so that we can bask in it and enjoy it.

According to this point of view, it is important to take into account the time needed to maintain the relationship of friendship with our Lord. Saint Ignatius, in Annotation 12 of his *Exercises*, notes that the soul must make sure that it has given God a sufficient amount of time. We must be encouraged, Lord, to make that prayerful request of the Lord even before beginning an act of thanksgiving, praise, or a contemplation of your mysteries. This time given over to God initially may be an hour, a half-hour, or fifteen minutes. It is freely given with no expectation of return. It is given for no other reason than for the pleasure of being with you. Or better yet, it is given solely because the Lord takes great pleasure in seeing you there, in his presence. Then, we must actually arrive. We keep our appointment. We perhaps have a spirit that is encumbered with worries and preoccupations; and we may be conscious that our prayer leaves a lot to be desired. But at least we come and we stay—in the same spirit as the poor child who had nothing to give, other than himself and his time. We could be sick; we could be tired; or we could have a spirit that resists all efforts at reflection. That doesn't matter! We will fill this time as we want. Or more often, as we are able, "throwing a few bits of kindling on the fire from time to time in order to keep it going," as Teresa says.

This is far from a difficult task. The business of friendship doesn't need a chief of protocol! Lord, you call us to an alliance that risks becoming an adventure. When, with Teresa, we understand what it is all about, we also solve, in a most elegant way, the problem of the connection between prayer and life. For what would a loving relationship be if it doesn't find a way to "just spend time" with the Beloved. How many relationships, founded on such great love, do not resist such treatment!

Without a doubt, the time spent in prayer is a question of vocation and situation. The amount of time spent by a Carmelite, a parish priest, or a mother are not necessarily the same. What is important is that they spend it. But, inversely, the business of friendship cannot be reduced to moments that are spent in heart-to-heart conversations. It happens all throughout the day, no matter what distance separates you from the Beloved.

Also, says Saint Teresa: "Don't be sad, sisters, when obedience takes you into the kitchen. The Lord walks among the pots and pans" (F, 5/8). Those who commit themselves to follow you, Lord, will know how and where to find you.

REFLECTION QUESTIONS

How do I maintain my friendship with God through prayer? Do I rely very much on formal creeds? Is my prayer too casual? Do I attempt to balance my prayer life with God by exploring different kinds of praying like I might balance my friendship with a close friend with different kinds of activities? Can I simply relax in the presence of God and just "be" with him?

DAY TWO

I Am Yours

FOCUS POINT

We were made to love God. God is the center of our lives—or, at least, he should be. We belong to God, not in some manner of enslavement—since we are given great freedom by our Creator—but rather as his sons and daughters. God is our *Father* in heaven, and we are truly complete, and we truly delight, when we are in his presence. Therefore, we try to give ourselves completely to him, without reservation. It is in this manner of giving that every part of our person experiences the delight of God's presence.

My confessors commanded me and gave me plenty of leeway to write about the favors and the kind of prayer the Lord has

granted me (Prologue to her autobiography in The Collected
Works of Teresa of Ávila, No. 1).

I am Yours and born for You,
What do You want from me?

Majestic Sovereign,
Unending wisdom,
Kindness pleasing to my soul;
God sublime, one Being Good,
Behold this one so vile.
Singing of her love to You:
What do You want of me?

Yours, You made me,
Yours, You saved me,
Yours, You endured me,
Yours, You called me,
Yours, You awaited me,
Yours, I did not stray.
What do You want of me?
(Po II, "In the Hands of God").

J ulian of Ávila was an amiable storyteller of the voyages of
the Holy Mother, and Teresa seemed to like to sing these
stanzas when he accompanied her on her journeys to set up
her foundations. The poem that is given above is part of the
longest and best known by Saint Teresa. While this poem is
characteristic of her way of prayer, at the same time, it poses
the fundamental question that all humans come to ask—either

at the moment of conversion, at the moment of choice of a state of life, or simply when one goes on a retreat, taking a step back with respect to what is urgent in order to turn oneself toward what is essential.

What do you want of me? Why have I come to this world? What is my place? What am I to do? Saint Ignatius invited his retreat participants to ask themselves the same question at the beginning of his *Exercises*. Teresa supplies an original response here: "I am Yours and born for You." She will find the reasons for her life by looking upon the Lord's initiatives. Perhaps this response is an unexpected one at first, but one which will finally echo Saint John's words in his first epistle: "In this is love, not that we loved God but that he loved us (first)(...). God is love, and those who abide in love abide in God, and God abides in them" (1 Jn 4:10, 16).

This answer is not a philosophical response but one that is about love's design and God's salvation. But, for each of us, this response must become concrete and operative in our lives. We must physically touch the initiatives of tenderness that God has given to us. Teresa considers her autobiography to be a recitation and a chronicle of the mercies of the Beloved for her.

The details that she gives us in the stanzas quoted at the beginning of this chapter is, at the same time, both classic and marked by a humor from which she never departs. "Yours, You have created me," she says. Saint Clare, one of the great heavenly friends of our saint, had already thanked the Lord in this way for having given her existence—the gift of existence, a gift that is constantly being renewed (the philosophers tell us). Is this gift not the most patent sign of God's mercy toward us? As an extension of that gift, one could say, would be the gift of redemption, salvation, and the call to follow Jesus closely. There are so many initiatives of tenderness which each take on a unique color and which we must remember in each of their different manifestations. Names, places, people, dates, and faces become precious to our memories in this way. They situate the events in which we learn to recognize the Lord's passage. Some of them appear to be signs to us, if we could manage to see that a certain coincidence of time and place is loaded with significance for us and our relationship with God. At times, we may only discover the significance later, when we attentively or lovingly go over certain events. This should not surprise us: the signs are often very personal; they only mean something to us, and it may, at times, even be an error to want to impose our convictions and interpretations on others. The grace of an event is addressed to each of us personally, and to no one else. Furthermore, the Lord only shows "his back" to us (Ex 33: 23). By the time we have perceived his presence, he is already gone, just as it was for the disciples at Emmaus.

Lord, that is why it is good for us, when we pause to reflect, or when we are in prayer, to do what was asked of Teresa. She reviewed the events of her life and figured out their meaning. It was not always easy for her. She knew that it was one thing to live what happens, another to understand what is lived, and still another to express it. Lord, you did not refuse, to whomever requested it, this grace to understand the favors which we have been granted, whether they are small or great. Besides, Scripture can help us to understand. A certain event in the gospel or another book on spiritual matters could act as a mirror that reveals God's initiatives of tenderness. Teresa always pursued this avenue with great realism, yet not without humor: "Yours, (...) You endured me; ...Yours, You awaited me, Yours, I did not stray." She was also conscious of her misery and of her delay in understanding, just as Saint Augustine wrote: "I loved you late, O Supreme Beauty."

But Lord, you are patient. You are patient because you are strong. You do not fail. You have drawn "the marvelous little girl" (as George Bernanos calls our Blessed Lady) that you destined to become the mother of your Son, from a long line of heroes and saints, but also from scoundrels, as the genealogy of the Gospel of Saint Matthew attests. Then, you know how to wait. You are not disconcerted by the weakness of human persons. Thérèse of Lisieux refused you nothing from the age of four. Teresa of Ávila would need ten times this to come to the same level.

When we understand this very simple truth, everything changes—just as the framework of a miserable life can be transformed by a ray of sunshine. The most elementary realities of each day, our daily bread, health, a place in the sun, the warmth of affection, and the very virtues we could show—all the things that we tend to regard as our due—now appear to be a gift from God's hand, from the Father as an initiative of tenderness. All that we have, and all that we are, we return to God through praise and thanksgiving. It is not a question of attributing any merits to ourselves, and even less of being vain about our positive qualities.

As well, we must also understand that we must take our turn and endure painful situations and "inescapable" obstacles with patience and self-abandon. Sad events are also full of significance. And your tenderness, O Lord, through which we have acquired assurance in view of its benefits, will draw something good for us out of the sadness and pain.

REFLECTION QUESTIONS

Do I give every part of who I am to God? What areas of my life are kept separate from God? My working life? My leisure time? Relationships with certain people in my life? How can I turn these areas of alienation into a "welcoming ground" for God's presence? Can I pray on this? Can I pray that I might be aware of when I am keeping out God's presence in my life so that I might be able to respond in ways that are welcoming and loving?

DAY THREE

Thrown Into Hell

FOCUS POINT

Teresa's vision of hell had an extraordinary impact on her life, as the following quotes of this saint will attest to. We may not experience such a harrowing vision ourselves, but we do get glimpses of the eternal loneliness and sadness that living without God promises. Those moments when we feel like God is far away from us are difficult—but ultimately beneficial to our friendship with God. Do I not miss my friend when he or she leaves town for a period of time? When I see that friend again, am I not more appreciative of the friendship we share? It is like this with God when our prayer is dry and he feels far away.

A long time after the Lord had already granted me many of the favors I've mentioned and other lofty ones, when I was in prayer one day, I suddenly found that, without knowing how, I had seemingly been thrown into hell. I understood that the Lord wanted me to see the place the devils had prepared there for me and which I merited because of my sins. The experience took place within the shortest space of time, but even were I to live for many years, I think it would be impossible for me to forget it. The entrance, it seems to me, was similar to a very long and narrow alleyway, like an oven, low, dark, and confined. The floor seemed to consist of dirty, muddy water emitting a foul stench, swarming with putrid vermin. At the end of the alleyway, a hole that looked like a small cupboard was hollowed out in the wall; there I found I was placed in a cramped condition. All of this was delightful to see in comparison with what I felt there.

What I described can hardly be exaggerated.

What I felt cannot even begin to be exaggerated; nor can it be understood. I experienced a fire in the soul that I don't know how I could describe. The bodily pains were so unbearable that though I suffered excruciating ones in this life and, according to what doctors say, the worst that can be suffered on earth (...), these were all nothing in comparison with the ones I experienced there, knowing that they would go on without end and never ceasing.

(...) To say the experience is as though the soul was continually being wrested from the body would be insufficient, for it would make you think somebody else is taking away your life, whereas here, it is the soul itself that is tearing itself to pieces.

(...) Afterwards, I saw another vision of frightful things, the punishment of some vices. This seemed much more fright-

ening to me, but since I didn't feel the pain, they didn't cause me as much fear. For in the former vision, the Lord wanted me actually to feel those spiritual torments and afflictions, as though the body was suffering them.

(…) I was left so terrified that, now, I am still frightened writing about this. (…) Thus I recall no time of trial or suffering without thinking that everything that can be suffered here on earth is nothing; so, I think, we complain without reason most of the time. This experience was one of the greatest favors the Lord granted me because it helped me a great deal to lose the fear of the tribulations and contradictions of this life as well as to grow strong enough to suffer them and give thanks to the Lord who, as it now appears, freed me from such everlasting and terrible evils (V, 32/ 1–4).

D oes the passage above represent a morbid vision? Does it represent a precious grace, because it is effective by instilling terror? Not in the least! We must not disregard this text. In spite of its questionable focus, it delivers a righteous perspective to us, not so much of sin, but of salvation—or, rather, of the condition of the redeemed sinner.

Let us note, at the onset, the time of the vision. Teresa had been receiving exceptional favors for a long time—for at least five or six years. For a great period of time she had known that she was loved by God and could not conceive of her life as being other than a welcome for this love. Now she can understand what the salvation that the Lord has given her consists of; she is able to measure the precious nature of her redemption. Thus, such a person, having narrowly escaped from mortal danger, could joyfully feel how good it is to be alive.

Without a doubt, Teresa's vision was an offshoot of the teachings of her times. It was also a consequence of her temperament: for a woman of such purity, such as Teresa was, everything she saw in this vision was dirty and repugnant; for a soul enamored with freedom, punishment is placement in "a small cupboard," a cramped condition. However, we note a theological perspective that is profoundly accurate: the soul tears itself apart, feeling it was made for God, having no other happiness than in him and, nevertheless, stuck in a wall of refusal in "the place the devils had prepared for me." We note that is was the devils, not the Lord, who lure souls into hell. But must we believe that each of us has a small cupboard awaiting us with our name on it? We can have our doubts! Wouldn't it be more appropriate to think, using this image-provoking language, that Teresa, who, without a doubt, never seriously sinned, became conscious of a presence within herself of the dynamic of evil and the logic of sin? She perceived this dynamic of evil, like a curve that she would follow all the way to its end, that is to say, all the way to the obstinate and willful refusal to participate in the goodness of divine friendship. It was not enough to say that she would have perceived it, but she told us she had lived it—and suffered it.

But she suffered it within the perspective of salvation. We must see the message that comes from these lines. It is not "Watch out, if you have sinned against me!" It is "Look from what an abyss I have saved you!" So that the fruits of this vision are, above all, a thanksgiving. The person who is open to the salvation that God proposes, discovers the dimension of the gift he has been given. Correlatively, without a doubt, the light of divine love makes him aware of his misery. It is a painful awareness, which could make tears flow, but one of recognition as much as of repentance and confusion.

At the same time, this awakening of conscience stimulates rather than paralyzes. We all know a person who has been cured of a fear of thunderstorms by passing time in the midst of one. Thus, Teresa understood that the problems here on earth are, according to the words of Saint Paul, without comparison to those which await us for eternity. Teresa translated that to mean: "Most of the time, we complain for nothing." Henceforth, her courage feeds off this certainty of being loved and delivered, as well as this awareness according to which "everything is nothing," in comparison to the one unique necessity.

Lord Jesus, it is good for us to understand, as does Teresa, what exactly is the misery from which you deliver us. In each of us there exists a dynamic of evil, an inclination for refusal. In us, this dynamic has deep roots: it could have its origins in our temperament, or our physiology; or it could be born out of psychological wounds from childhood; it could even be the result of a good quality that could oppose, one could speculate, our own grace. So it is, for example, with the dynamism of a complex nature which makes us less attentive to the weakness of others. More than deeds done, this dynamic constitutes "our fundamental sin." For each of us, it has its particular color, just as, from a young age, each of us has our own way of saying no: caressing, charming, raging, obstinate, calm, or provocative; this dynamic has all the differing nuances. Let this dynamism grow in us, and it will devour everything and lead us to the obstinate refusal of God, of others and of ourselves in our fundamental calling. Lord, it is from these circumstances that we have to be saved.

Oh! Without a doubt, it is against this eventuality that we must fight: to correct ourselves, as we say. But this effort—a necessary one—remains inadequate. Lord, it is you who saves us. Saint Ignatius rightfully says that all regard for oneself must end in a conversation with the Merciful One, accompanied by a glance at the Crucified One!

And when you save someone, Lord, things generally pass in a reverse order: it is love that you first kindle in the soul. It is this love that makes one aware of one's own misery and sin and ends in the ability to sustain intolerable suffering. The suffering of purgatory, which is purifying and sanctifying, is destined to transform itself into a thanksgiving.

"Yours, You saved me; Yours, I did not stray," says Saint Teresa finally.

REFLECTION QUESTIONS

How do I feel when my prayer life becomes dry and God is seemingly absent from my life? How do I respond to this feeling? Is my faith shaken or made stronger? What do thoughts of hell bring to my mind? Do thoughts of hell fill me with shame and despair, or do these thoughts increase my gratitude for the saving acts of Jesus Christ? Am I aware of choices in my life—choices that bring me closer to God and choices that lead me away from him? How do these choices/habits affect feelings of loneliness and alienation from God?

DAY FOUR

Devoted to the Glorious Mary Magdalene

FOCUS POINT

When we come to the realization that we are human beings with fault there are several forks in the road that draw our attention: we can decide that we have the power to save ourselves, and by our own efforts reach salvation; we can despair, convinced that not even God can save us from our sorry state; or we can throw ourselves on God's mercy, trusting that he—and only he—has the power to save us. It is the latter choice that is correct, of course. Realizing our faults and our sinfulness is a good thing. It can lead us to God once we recognize that only through God can salvation occur.

Well, my soul now was tired; and, in spite of its desire, my wretched habits would not allow it rest. One day, upon entering the oratory, I saw a statue they had borrowed for a certain feast to be celebrated in the house. It showed the much wounded Christ and inspired so much devotion that the sight of it troubled me, for it so well represented what he had suffered for us. I felt so keenly aware of how poorly I had thanked him for those wounds that my heart broke. Beseeching him to strengthen me, once and for all, so that I might no longer offend him, I threw myself down before him in a torrent of tears.

I was very devoted to the glorious Mary Magdalene and frequently thought about her conversion, especially when I received Holy Communion. For since I knew the Lord was certainly present there within me, I, thinking that he would not despise my tears, placed myself at his feet. And I didn't know what I was saying (he did a great favor by allowing me to shed them for him, since I so quickly forgot these regrets); and I commended myself to this glorious saint that she might obtain pardon for me.

But this latter instance with the statue had a greater effect upon me, for I was very distrustful of myself and placed all my trust in God. I think I then said to him that I would not rise from there until he granted what I was begging him for. I truly believe that this was beneficial to me, because from that time on, I changed a great deal (V, 9/1–3).

T his event probably took place in 1554. Teresa was approaching the age of forty. Ever since the death of her father, some ten years earlier, she had not abandoned prayer. In the community, we justly see her as a model religious. However, she was not satisfied. She saw too many imperfections and bad habits in herself that left a lot to be desired. She wanted to please the Lord in everything and refuse him nothing. But she felt that she would never reach this end on her own. Then, like the sinner in the gospel in whom, with all of those of her era, she recognized to be Mary Magdalene, she threw herself at the feet of the Lord and begged him to turn the page for her, which she could not do for herself.

We will make two further comments with respect to this important event in Teresa's life. First, it is God who gives salvation, not man through his own efforts. Then, this God that saves, for Teresa, as for all Christians, is "the Good Jesus." As Matthew says: "You are to name him Jesus, for he will save his people from their sins" (Mt 1:21).

This God saves the whole person and removes him from his misery. I am the salvation of my people, said the Lord. No matter what the problem is that causes them to call upon me, I will hear them. When Jesus announced the kingdom in the gospel, he gave signs of it by saving people from all sorts of difficulties: the wedding couple in Cana, from a minor catastrophe; and the people who followed him into the desert, from hunger; the sick, from all kinds of physical ailments or, as we now call them, psychological or psychosomatic ones. He even removed the dead from their rest. Without a doubt, these are only temporary victories. The definitive triumph over all evil will come from his own Resurrection. But his victories are signs: physical distress and even death will not have the last word for human beings.

Jesus always saved by attacking the root of evil. That root is to be found in the human heart and it is called sin. Jesus did not procure a physical recovery without it being accompanied by a healing of the heart: as he told the paralyzed man, "Take heart, son; your sins are forgiven" (Mt 9:2). Inversely, many moral healings and conscience corrections also provided happy consequences for the psyche and even the physical being.

But we must take this consideration a step further if we want to become aware of the total dimension of the salvation that Christ brings. For, according to the insightful remarks made by André Malraux (a student of Christian iconography during the troubled periods of the Hundred Years War and the Black Death), we then see images of devils appear, as if human beings become aware that the action of good and evil had certain dimensions that were beyond the merely human. This is true: man is engaged in a battle that is bigger than he is. And it is Jesus who hunts the devils. No matter what theological interpretations we could give to these episodes, they show that Jesus remained in control, including control of those things which Saint Paul called "the forces." It is then from the strength of the Lord that man would be delivered from all dimensions.

Must we also make plain that the Lord never saves in an automatic manner? He respects us too much not to make us instruments associated with our own salvation. When he promised the land of Canaan to his people, he did not agree to let it fall into their hands without any effort. "I promise you will inherit the land of Canaan" means: "I promise you the courage necessary to conquer it." So that, at the end of our lives, we will be able to state that salvation is, at its human level, our all, and, at its level of grace, God's all.

This work of salvation brings with it a certain number of consequences to which, Lord Jesus, we do not pay enough attention. First, you teach us to be patient. We cannot make a plant grow by pulling on its leaves. It takes time for fruit to reach maturity. It accomplishes nothing to force the process.

In the same way, we do not reach the stature of a perfect person in Christ overnight. Lord, you are patient with us because you are strong and you know that you have to wait until your time. And ours.

And then, Lord, teach us not to be upset at the difference in time that exists between spiritual conversion and psychological conversion. We are not angels. The spirit is quick, but the flesh is slow and weak. After receiving grace before your image, Teresa consciously and voluntarily refused you nothing. You could say, she did it cold.

But there remains certain friendships which, although good and not offensive to you, still hold too great a place in her life. A great effort will be made on her part to get rid of them. It will be in vain, until you intervene yourself, Lord. As Teresa says: "I had so much sorrow when I renounced it (ridding myself of it) like it was something that seemed inconvenient to me; but that day, the Lord gave me the strength and the freedom to act" (V, 24/7). Everything has its own time. And right to the end of our days, we will have weaknesses and imperfections caused by our miseries, fragility, and psychological wounds. The ideal of Christian perfection is not one of a statue without faults, but one of a human being, carried by love, who answers you, Lord, love for love.

Yet this misery itself which still dwells within us in spite of our efforts and makes us suffer, is excellent food for the fire of love. Lord, to ask you to pardon one of our weaknesses that makes us fail, more or less involuntarily, is to tell you again that we love you. When we have reached that point, the Adversary no longer has a grip: our very faults are the proof of our progress in love. It is to say that your hold becomes total, that you take the reins of our existence yourself and you completely deserve the name of Savior in our eyes.

REFLECTION QUESTIONS

How do I respond when my sinfulness takes hold of my attention? Do I despair? Am I depressed? Or am I aware enough to recognize this as an ideal opportunity to give my fears and worries over to God? How does this dependence and allowance of God taking over make me feel? Closer to God? When I rely more on God and consider his great mercy, am I more willing to forgive others who have hurt me?

DAY FIVE

No Better Friend
Than Christ

FOCUS POINT

Saint Teresa—like many saints—had a very special relationship with Jesus Christ. Jesus was her friend. Not "friend" in
the manner of acquaintance, but "friend" in the deepest sense.
Her understanding of Jesus as a friend made it emotionally
difficult to accept the fact that he had to suffer and die for the
sake of our salvation. How blessed would we all be if we understood Jesus as a friend to this degree! Our time is precious
to us, and we choose to spend so much of our time with friends.
If Jesus is truly our friend, then it only makes sense that we
would want to spend as much time as possible in his presence.

I saw that he was a man, even though he was God; that he wasn't surprised by the weaknesses of men; that he understands our miserable make-up, subject to many falls because of the original sin, which he came to repair. I can speak with him as with a friend, even though he is the Lord (...) (V, 37/5).

Treat him as a father, a brother, a master, and a husband, once one way, another time in another way. He will teach you himself what you must do to please him (C, 8/3).

All my life I had been greatly devoted to Christ (...). My devotion for him was extreme. (...) And I then returned to my habit of continually rejoicing in the company of the Lord, especially when I was taking Communion. I would have liked to have had his portrait or image always before my eyes, since I could not have it as deeply engraved in my soul as I would have liked. Is it possible, my Lord, that for so much as an hour, I could have entertained the thought that you could have hindered my greatest good? From where have all these good things come to me, if not from you? (...) (V, 22/4).

It is through this Lord of ours that all blessings come. He will show us the way; we must look at his life—that is our best model. What more do we need than to have, at our side, such a good Friend who will not leave us in trials and tribulations, as earthly friends do? Blessed is he who loves him in truth and has him always at his side. Let us consider the glorious Saint Paul, from whose lips the name of Jesus never seems to have been absent, because he was firmly enshrined in his heart. Since realizing this, I have looked carefully at the lives of a number of saints who were great contemplatives, and I find that they followed exactly the same road. Saint Francis with his stigmata, illustrates this, as does Saint Anthony of Padua with the Divine Infant. Saint Bernard, too, delighted in Christ's humanity, and so did Saint Catherine of Siena and many others (...) (V, 22/7).

I believe I've explained how important it is for souls, however spiritual, to take care not to flee from corporal things to the extent of thinking that even the most Holy Humanity causes harm. Some quote what the Lord said to his disciples that it was fitting that he go. I can't bear this (6D, 7/14).

—————

W hat does Teresa repent for in this passage from Chapter 22 cited above? It is the key chapter of her doctrine that she more concisely repeats in *The Interior Castle* (6D, 7). Under the influence of certain masters of prayer, Teresa had believed, for some time, that she had been practicing the technique "mental void," by trying to imitate, through her own efforts, this suspension of psychological activities that God grants in supernatural prayer. In this context, the Holy Humanity of the Lord must, as all other created mediations, be set aside. We are not lacking renowned spiritual authors who advocate this attitude by using the words of Jesus after the Last Supper in support of their thesis: "it is to your advantage that I go away" (Jn 16: 7).

Teresa comes back to this concept in *The Interior Castle*:

I realized clearly that I was proceeding badly (...). I didn't understand the reason, nor would I have understood it, in my opinion (...), until a person with whom I was discussing my prayer, who was a servant of God, warned me (6D, 7/15).

Who is this servant of God? Perhaps it was Saint Peter of Alcantara or Saint Francis Borgia. It could simply have been Father Diego of Cetina, the first Jesuit she spoke to. Her friends in Ávila, although they had been slightly exposed to theology, were at a loss. They advised her to call upon one of the religious from the new Company, which was founded by Father Ignatius of Loyola, who had just established themselves at the San Gil college. Thus, a young priest of twenty-five came to her; he had been recently ordained and had talents in which the superiors of the Company only granted moderate confidence. A servant of God, he clearly saw what others had not seen there, he understood Teresa to be this "monument" of extraordinary graces. He prescribed to her, as a doctor does when he makes out a prescription, to stop each day and think about a detail in the passion (V, 23/17).

If the truth be told, Father Diego preached to a converted sinner. Teresa told us this herself: "All my life I had been greatly devoted to Christ." Even when she was a small child in her father's house, she often stopped to gaze at an image of Jesus meeting the woman from Samaria. She saw herself as the Samaritan woman, before Jesus, who promised her living water. Later, she would see herself as Veronica, so wanting to wipe the Face of the Lord and his painful perspirings, at the time of his agony. She would always have, as a model, Mary Magdalene seated at the feet of the Lord, welcoming his message and making homage to him with a heart that listens.

For Teresa says: "I saw that he was a man, even though he was God." Her religion was an "incarnated" one. The God she addressed herself to was the God with a human face, the one who became the carpenter from Nazareth for us through love. The little girl who "wanted to see God" never aspired— except for a few months when she followed the path of "no pensar nada"—to see him in any other way than in this Holy Humanity which was the necessary path. She had nothing in common with either the Eastern or Western mystics who advocated a method of direct contact with "the Divine." A Christian, she learned to love "the Good Jesus" and, from her childhood, all the way to the Seven Dwellings, she knew no other God. It was in him that she has "access in one Spirit to the Father" (Eph 2:18).

From this came her naive practices, not only when she made her intense search, but also later, when the Lord would have definitively seized her life. In 1571, she noted:

> For more than thirty years I have taken Communion on this day (Palm Sunday). (…) I feel that the Jews had shown themselves to be very cruel by letting him eat so far away after having received him so solemnly, and I sought to keep him in me, in a place which, I can now see, left much to be desired. These were my naive considerations (…) (FVD, Ávila, April 1572).

From this way of knowing also came her familiar speaking about him as a traveling companion along the road, whose association brought her a knowledge of him that is both intimate and concrete at the same time. "My God is not susceptible. (…) He is not scrupulous, but magnanimous (…). He gives many rewards. He rewards scrupulously, broadly (…). He doesn't like it if we worry too much about speaking to him." These expressions that are notably interspersed in *The Way of Perfection* show both who Teresa's Jesus is and who is Teresa of Jesus.

We are at the end of a long story that we must soon evaluate with her. But, from now on, let us allow ourselves to be guided by her teachings. "Master, who are you?" This question does not call upon the answer, which we recited by heart, from the little catechism; no more than the knowledge of the Christological councils. She waits for an existential answer: "You are the one I gave myself to: the one who made me what I am." So that we cannot justify the hope that is within us—to say who is the Lord—without involving ourselves and giving witness to our own history which we live in concert with our Lord.

But before this history of ours can begin—or can begin again in a new stage—we must remember this covenant to which the Master calls us: "If you want to, come, follow me." And we must reply: "I will follow you, Lord, wherever you may go. For better or worse. I will stay with you like Mary Magdalene, seated at your feet, or be your chosen vase like Paul. In the hidden solitude of Ávila or along the roads of the foundations."

Moreover, keeping company with the Master is never purely platonic. It calls for deeds. Teresa worked for and with Jesus. Each of her foundations was her way of gaining glory for this Lord; this glory could only be promoted by founding another eucharistic presence, by offering herself in homage to the religious and the faithful. How many times, stricken with fever, suffering in pain in all of her limbs, had she not found renewed vigor and dynamism through the simple thought that she was serving this good Master? As an example, let us take a citation about the foundation of the community at Palencia:

> The devil and illness held me bound (…). Our Lord answered in a kind of reprehensive way: "What do you fear? When have I failed you? (…)." O great God! How different are your words from those of men! I was

thereby left with such determination and courage that the whole world would not have been enough to oppose me. I began at once to make arrangements (F, 29/6).

Lord, if one day you decide, if you want, when you want, to speak to me, I must, from now on, begin to seriously seek you. "Where do you dwell?" Andrew and John asked you this when they followed you. It is the question that I again ask of you today. Where do you dwell? That is to say, where can I find you in the concrete condition of my own existence? What is the step you are asking me to take now in your direction?

REFLECTION QUESTIONS

Do I perceive God as a friend? If not, how can I cultivate this friendship to the degree of joy which Saint Teresa knew as a friend of God? If I do perceive God as a friend, in what ways do express my friendship to him? Do I seek to spend time with God as I do with my other friends? It is said that the friends we keep say very much about who we are and what we strive to become as people. In what ways does this hold true for my relationship with God?

DAY SIX

After Seeing the Lord's Great Beauty

FOCUS POINT

There are times when I recognize feelings of jealousy toward a saint. I am envious that a saintly man or woman has experienced Jesus Christ in an extraordinary manner, while I have not. Teresa most assuredly dealt with jealous and envious people in her own life, after she experienced Jesus in the mystical manner of a vision. More often that not, these feelings of jealousy and envy are temporary, and they soon pass, making room for admiration and awe, and creating a place where others can seek guidance and spiritual aid from the one who was so blest.

Returning to the account of my life, (…) and the prayers that were being made for me so that the Lord would lead me by another and a surer way, since, as they told me, there was so much doubt about the one I was following (…).

At the end of two years, during which time both other people and myself were continually praying for what I have described—that the Lord would either lead me by another way or make the truth evident to me (…). One day, when I was at prayer on the glorious feast day of Saint Peter, I saw Christ at my side—or to put it better, I was conscious of him, for neither with the eyes of the body, nor with those of the soul did I see it was he who, as I thought, was speaking to me. Not knowing that visions of this kind could occur, I was very afraid at first, and did nothing but weep, but, as soon as he addressed a single word to reassure me, I regained my composure and was quite happy and free from fear. Jesus Christ seemed to be beside me all of the time, but, as this was not an imaginary vision, I could not discern in what form: I clearly felt that he was always at my right side, and a witness to everything I was doing (V, 27/1–2).

One day, while I was in prayer, the Lord wanted to show me only his hands which were so very beautiful, I would be unable to exaggerate the beauty (…). A few days later, I also saw that divine face which it seems left me completely absorbed. (…) One feast day of Saint Paul, while I was at Mass, this most Holy Humanity in its risen form showed himself to me completely (…) (V, 28/1–3).

The Lord almost always showed Himself to me as risen, also when he appeared in the Host—except at times when he showed me his wounds in order to encourage me when I was suffering

tribulation. Sometimes, he appeared on the cross or in the gar-
den [of Olives], and a few times with the crown of thorns;
sometimes he also appeared carrying the cross because, as I
say, of my needs and those of others, but his body was always
glorified (V, 29/4).

N ow, we must follow Teresa in her long adventure with Jesus. It is now January 1560, or perhaps June of the same year. The first experience of Christ's presence that Teresa speaks about here is not just a simple happening in among others in the list of her mystical graces. It is situated in a dynamic whose design elicits our admiration. Our saint had sought the company of the Lord for a long time. And here, after the scene of the wounded Christ in 1554, Jesus came to meet her: tenderly, progressively, as if to court the Beloved. First he gave her the grace of supernatural prayer, in which she seemed enraptured by a mysterious force. Then he made her listen—interiorly, not like the voices of Joan of Arc—to the words from the Scriptures. She didn't doubt the divine origin of these experiences. Moreover, she saw herself as the tree for his fruit: the progress she had made in retreats, peace, and charity are there to give witness. But these graces were accompanied by ecstasies which became public and caused her to be suspected of having illusions or diabolical possession. So, those around her had doubts: not only in the small religious world of Ávila, which took sides for and against her, but even her confessors and consultors did not know what to believe. This controversy caused her to suffer a thousand deaths. She prayed, and we pray with her, so that it would become clear. And here, just as to Saul on the road to Damascus, Jesus replied. There was total disagreement between Stephen and Saul: Stephen died having seen Jesus at the right hand of God (Acts 7:55) and Jesus said to Saul: Stephen was right, "I am Jesus, whom you are persecuting" (Acts 9:5). Teresa prayed in this same way so that the truth would come out. And Jesus replied. In his own way.

This reply, like all divine favors, was given to her "for her service." In Teresa's life, it was the equivalent of the inaugural visions of an Isaiah, a Jeremiah, or an Ezekiel, prophets from either the Old or New Testaments. Teresa is constituted a witness of the Christian experience. She will have a mission to proclaim to the people of God: "This presence of the risen Lord which we believe through faith is not a decoy. I met the Lord, I experienced and felt his presence."

It was only an inaugural experience, but it would develop more fully later. While the Lord had made both Ezekiel and Saint John devour the book of the Word, at the time of the Spanish Inquisition, when they banned the religious books written in the popular language of the time, the Lord was happy to promise Teresa: "Have no fear, my daughter, I will give you a living book" (V, 26/5). This book now opens its pages before her.

For a dozen years, Teresa would be granted frequent experiences of the presence of Jesus. These presences were accompanied by visions in images: furtive visions and rapid visions, yet all were interior—she did not see them with her eyes as did Bernadette of Lourdes—but with an extraordinary brilliance, charged with an unsuspected depth of significance. At times, she was also granted visions of the Lord which we might characterize as intellectual and savory comprehensions, although they were still limited, of the most unsolvable mysteries, such as that of the Holy Trinity. The Lord, as a truly living book, would instruct her himself. And, in an almost unique case in the history of mysticism, he illuminated her with the totality of the revealed information that was known in her time: starting from the Trinity all the way down to the virtues of holy water (V, 32/4), as one of her critics would jokingly say.

Thus, when she wrote, as ordered by her confessors, about the graces she had received, Teresa became a witness of the highest order. We could say she was a prophet. For, according to the renowned words of Bergson, she conveyed the letters of dogma with characters of fire. Teresa, naturally very persuasive, became both a prophet and a teacher of the Church. Whoever became involved in her recitation of her adventure was warmed, if not enflamed, along with her.

And it was truly an adventure that occurred, in the loving sense of the word. From then on, a constant companionship developed between Teresa and Jesus. He manifested himself to Teresa when he wanted to: to reassure her, encourage her, enlighten her and, at times, to reprimand her (and then, she said that she didn't know "where to hide"). He accompanied her, followed at her side (she specified it was on her right side). He was the same companion for her as he was for the pilgrims of Emmaus or for the fishermen of the lake. He was also the Rabbouni of Mary Magdalene, and, just as that figure did, quickly disappeared. In Teresa's opinion, it was too quick, as she wished to see those incidents of Tabor last forever; yet she had only haste for one thing: to die in order to indefinitely unite herself with him.

All of these events happened between 1560 and 1572, at the time when Teresa undertook the reform of Carmel and its first foundations. Her interior adventure never prevented her from having her feet firmly planted on the ground. Nevertheless, she was torn within herself, just as was Saint Paul, who wanted to die with Christ and who also understood that the necessity of his mission forced him to be available for the people of God (see Phil 1:21–22).

Teresa would come to know a similar evolution. On November 18, 1572, she heard Jesus tell her: "Nothing could separate you from me (…). You will be my wife. My honor is yours, your honor is mine" (FVD). Later, she reported the same event but in more succinct terms: "Take care of my business and I will take care of yours" (7D, 2/1). This time, the tension was resolved. Teresa was no longer the beloved fiancée who had been foolishly smitten. She was the wife, in calm possession of her happiness. Marriage is forever. From then on, everything was shared with Jesus, honor as well as business. The idyllic part of the adventure would fade in order to leave room for a life that would, above all, become a work for two.

During the ten years that remained in her life, Teresa would not again know the extraordinary mystical experiences. Jesus no longer manifested himself at her side, but in the very depth of her soul, where the Holy Trinity lived. She was the shoot of the vine. He was the vine, their work was the same. Teresa of Jesus did Jesus' work, but she marked it with her own ingenuity: whether it was her foundations, or her tenacity through illness or trials, or her correspondence, or the writing of her major work, *The Interior Castle*. The definitive Teresa was not the one who was immortalized by Bernini, in rapture under the arrow of the cherub, but an active woman who united herself with both Martha and Mary Magdalene and dwelled with her Lord all the way among the pots and pans.

Lord, what can we do with this marvelous story of love? Envy the graces that Teresa received? The graces are not holiness. If you gave them to her it was for our edification: so that we will run toward you as she did, enveloped in the aroma of your perfumes. So that we also understand, from a woman truly alive—and not a statue—the truths that she touched with her fingers and so that we keep ourselves "in the obscurity" of faith. So that, in particular, we grasp, according to Saint Paul's teachings, that the mystery of the risen Christ is too rich to be exhausted in a single formula; and so that Christian life, according to the two stages lived by Teresa, is a life *with* Christ as a traveling companion, and *in* Christ through this mysterious belonging to his Body.

Moreover, Lord, at times, we are granted, in prayer or outside of it, certain favors which warm our hearts. A certain verse of Scripture, read twenty times, reveals itself, this time, as having expressed everything to us; a certain detail of an evangelical scene appears to bring us enlightenment, dynamism, joy, and peace to a level that had been unsuspected until then. Are these equivalent to Teresa's visions? The theologian would surely introduce certain distinctions of degree and even of nature. But you gave us a few crumbs of desire for the feast that you granted to your beloved Teresa. And we precisely recognize them as such because her experience acts on our own as a "magnifying mirror."

May you be blessed, Lord, for having brought Teresa's adventure of love to us, not to awaken jealousy in us, but to enlighten and stimulate us on this way of union with you in faith where you also await us.

REFLECTION QUESTIONS

How do I respond to those people who encounter Jesus Christ in a very special way? Am I envious? Am I jealous? Do I doubt the authenticity of their experience? Am I happy for this person? Do I seek out this person and attempt to gain some insight into spiritual living as a result of their experience? Am I present to that person as they attempt to deal with the special and holy encounter with which they have been graced?

DAY SEVEN

Converse Not With Men,
But With Angels

FOCUS POINT

God demands all of our love, and we attempt to give him every bit of it. Of course, we love others in our life—family, friends, even strangers. How can this be, if we try to give all of our love to the Lord? We love others because we see the love they have for God within them. We are loving their loving God; we are loving God through their loving God. In this manner, all of our love is directed toward God, as all of our love for others is simply love for God who we see within them.

For my soul was far from being strong, but it was very sensitive, especially with respect to abandoning certain friendships

40

which were not actually leading me to offend God (...). He (my confessor) told me to commend the matter to God for a few days, and to recite the hymn "Veni, Creator," so that he would enlighten me as to what was the best thing to do. One day, when I spent a long time in prayer, beseeching the Lord to help me please him in everything, (...) I was seized by a rapture that was so sudden that it almost carried me away (...). That was the first time I heard these words: "I no longer want you to converse with men, but with angels."

(...) The words have come true; never since that time have I been able to maintain a solid friendship except with people who I believe love God and try to serve him, nor have I derived comfort from anyone else or cherished any private affection for them (V, 24/5–6).

I had a serious fault that did me great harm; it was that when I began to know that certain persons liked me, and I found them attractive, I became so attached to them that my mind was bound strongly by the thought of them. There was no intention to offend God, but I was happy to see these persons, think about them, and about the good things I saw in them (...). After having seen the great beauty of the Lord, no one, in comparison with him, seemed to attract me or occupy my thoughts (...). I obtained such freedom in this respect that everything I see here below seems loathsome when compared to the excellent and beautiful qualities I saw in the Lord. There is no knowledge or any kind of gift that I think could amount to anything when compared with what it is to hear just one word spoken from that divine mouth (V, 37/4).

I am always very fond of those who guide my soul; as they so truly represented God to me and since I felt secure, I showed them that I liked them. They, as God-fearing servants of the Lord, were afraid that I would become attached to them in any way, and bound to this love, even in a holy way, and they showed me their displeasure (...). I laughed to myself to see how mistaken they were, although I didn't always clearly express just how little attached I was to anyone. But I assured them; and as they got to know me better, they realized what I owed to the Lord (V, 37/5).

W e can appreciate the Paulist flavor (see Phil 3:4–14) of this passage about the great beauty of the Lord. We may also note that the words heard in Teresa's joy in the Lord are an echo of the same Saint Paul (see Phil 3:20) in the Latin translation that was known to her: "But our conversation is with heaven." Our Doctor thus unites herself with the teachings of Saint John of the Cross: in the face of "everything" which is God's beauty, the remainder, no matter how respectable it is, counts for "nothing." In particular, the most precious of friendships pale.

Teresa had always been very gifted for the "business of friendship." As a young girl and as a young religious, she had been the magnet in both her family home as well as the convent of the Incarnation. This disposition had brought her, after a time, to a certain dissipation: dangerous friendships if not to her virtue, at least for her retreat from the world. She was so very attractive for honest people that they felt her great purity, her inability for the least bit of compromise with respect to honor, and, later, for her attachment to the Lord. It is not surprising that two or three years after her definitive conversion she was still taken with friendships which certainly didn't offend God, but which held too much importance. "There was a great deal of affection, but if I abandoned them, would I be sinning through ingratitude?" (V, 25/5).

However, this God that conquered her was a jealous God. He wanted all the space in Teresa's heart. She wanted to "satisfy him in everything." She prayed, she made the effort to rid herself of these friendships to the point of making herself sick (V, 24/7). She could not do it and finally renounced her attempts as being something that caused no problems (V, 24/7). We must not minimize Teresa's efforts. She wasn't lacking in generosity but in the light of discernment. That is why her confessor of the time, Father Juan de Pradanos, commanded her to invoke the Holy Spirit.

The Holy Spirit intervened with the speed of lightning. In an instant, he delivered her from what she could not distance herself from in her "active night." He made her renounce this friendship which was not evil, and put everything else in its proper place, according to the directions of her confessor.

We must stop at this episode. It is laden with meaning. Here, Teresa is like the rich young man in the gospel: "If you want to be perfect, sell all that you have and give the proceeds to the poor." What does she have? Teresa, who took a vow of poverty, still had the riches of her heart. And this is what the Lord asked of her, as he did of Abraham when he asked him to sacrifice his only son. He asked Teresa to pass her affective life by a kind of zero point; to accept, in all truth, that, if the Lord asked it of her, she would longer have any human friendships, nor would she have any loving dealings with humans, only with angels, those beings of faith.

Let us note that, at the time of this call, Jesus had not yet manifested himself to her. It was a dive into faith that was asked of her, a total abandonment to the whims of the Beloved. But the words that she heard were "substantial words," said John of the Cross. In an instant, Teresa saw that she must stop seeking all personal gratifications of the heart. And thus, her heart was freed.

Does this mean that she no longer knew the joy of human affection? At the very time that she related these facts, neither Father Jerome Gratien, nor Mary of Saint Joseph, nor John of the Cross, nor Anne of Jesus, nor any others had crossed her path! But nothing would be as it had been before. Jesus had seized all of her strength to love. If she felt affection for any-one from that time on, it was through the love—beginning or well advanced—that she discovered in this person for the One who was her only love. The affection that she gave witness to—the "good feeling" manifested to her confessors must not have been considered insignificant for someone as gifted!—is nothing more than the affection that is exchanged between herself and Jesus. It is Jesus whom she loves in this person. It is Jesus who loves through her.

But Jesus did not empty Teresa. Grace transforms the na-ture, it does not kill it; the affectionate Teresa, full of good feelings, thoughtful—"One could bribe me with a sardine!"—gave the entirety of her heart, just as she gave the entirety of her intelligence and her know-how. She succeeded in main-taining, with each of her friends—male or female—a unique relationship with an appropriateness that is nothing short of genius: all we have to do is to read her correspondence to be convinced of this fact.

We know of her affection for Father Gratien, to the point that they made up one of the most renowned saintly couples known throughout the history of the Church: Saint Francis and Saint Clare, and Saint Francis de Sales and Saint Jeanne de Chantal, for example. She kept up correspondence with the prioress of Seville, Mary of Saint Joseph, which explains the nuances of the most intimate and free friendships. She also prayed for Father Garcia of Toledo, her censor for the books *The Life* and *The Way of Perfection*: "Lord, consider it convenient that this man is our friend!" (V, 34/8). Fifteen years later, when the same Father Garcia came back from America, she wrote to the prioress of Seville: "Show him a great deal of friendship, treat him as if he was one of the founders of this order, he helped me so much; then, for him, don't veil your face [in the parlor—for visits]: but for the others, yes, especially for the Discalced!" (Letter of November 8, 1581).

We see that affection did not make the foundress lose her head! Perhaps she explains it crudely at times. Father Banez, to whom she had demonstrated many good feelings, neglected her somewhat...in favor of Maria Bautista, the prioress of Valladolid and Teresa's cousin. The Mother Superior wrote to her: "Know that these attentions for you will last until they fall on another that pleases him. Do not be afraid. He will be like this in spite of your presumption" (Letter of November 8, 1576). We can be holy and still keep certain feelings that are very...feminine!

From then on, Teresa saw each person in the light of Christ and, through that lens, she appreciated each for what they were. But to reach that point, she had to encounter the paschal mystery of death and resurrection—the death that is created by the night, even if it only lasts as long as a flash. In our era of cultural diversity, when the opportunities for privileged relationships are numerous, God does not want to kill affection, but he doesn't want them to compete with his own affection, once he has reserved a heart for himself.

"Lord, you created us for yourself, and our heart is without rest when it doesn't rest in you." We can make this prayer from Saint Augustine our own. Lord, see to it that the obstacles on our path are pushed aside so that, no matter what the legitimate sparks of our heart are, they can find rest in you.

REFLECTION QUESTIONS

When I am with my friends and family (even those people I do not know very well) am I aware of the love for God inside of them? If I am aware of this love they have for God, how do I respond? Am I more drawn to this loving person? Do I find it easier to "be with God" when I am in the presence of this person? In my own life, do I attempt to love God with every aspect of my being, in every arena of my life? How can I bring this potential to love God in all ways to a greater reality? What areas of my life—and what relationships with others—could benefit from greater loving on my part?

DAY EIGHT

I Insist on Three Things

FOCUS POINT

Life is most special when it is simplified, without complexity and confusion. Those elements that make life worth living are available to everyone of us, and if we are open to having them, God will bring them to us in abundance. Saint Teresa recognized this truth, and prayed that God's grace be given to her that she might have those three simple things (love for others, detachment from things, and true humility) that make a person truly happy and fulfilled. In the same way, we pray that God's grace enter our lives and give us those simple and important "three things" that will fill our lives with joy.

Before you say anything about interior matters, that is, about prayer, I shall mention some things that are necessary for those who seek to follow the way of prayer (...).

Do not think, my friends and daughters, that I shall burden you with many things; please God, we shall do what our holy fathers established and observed (...). I shall insist on only three things, which are from our own constitutions (...). The first of these is love for one another; the second is detachment from all created things; the third is true humility, which, even though I speak of it last, is the main practice and embraces all the others.

About the first, love for one another, it is most important that we have this, for there is nothing annoying that is not suffered easily by those who love one another—a thing would have to be extremely annoying before causing any displeasure. And if this commandment were observed in the world as it should be, I think such love would be very helpful for the observance of the other commandments. But, because of either excess or defect, we never reach the point of observing the commandment perfectly.

It may seem that having excessive love among ourselves could not be evil, but such excess carries with it so much evil and so many imperfections that I don't think anyone will believe this except someone who has been an eyewitness.

(...) For when love is in the service of his Majesty, the will does not proceed with passion, but proceeds by seeking help to conquer other passions (...). I would like there to be many of these friendships in a large community, but in this house, where there are no more than thirteen—nor must there be any more—everyone must be friends, everyone must be loved, everyone must be held dear, everyone must be helped. Watch out for these friendships, for love of the Lord (...) (C, 4/3–7).

Now, in the case of perfect love, if a person loves, there is the passion to make the other soul worthy of being loved, for this person knows that otherwise, he will not continue to love the other. It is a love that costs dearly. This person does everything he can for the other's benefit; he would lose a thousand lives so that a little good might come to the other soul. O precious love that imitates the Commander-in-Chief of love, Jesus, our Good! (C, 6/9).

Now, then, the first thing we must strive for is to rid ourselves of our love for our bodies, for some of us are by nature such lovers of comfort that there is a great deal of work to do in this area. And we are so fond of our health that it is amazing what a war our bodies cause, especially with religious and even with those who are not. But some religious it seems, including my-self, did not come to the monastery for any other reason than to strive not to die; each one strives for this as best she can. Here, truthfully, there is little opportunity to do this in deed, but I wouldn't want there to be even the desire. Be resolved to it, Sisters, that you came to die for Christ, not to live comfort-ably for Christ (C, 10/5).

Now, realize that anyone who doesn't know how to set up the pieces for a game of chess won't know how to play well (...). And oh, how permissive this kind of game will be for us; and how quickly, if we play it often, will we checkmate this divine King, who will not be able to escape, nor will he want to.

The queen is the piece that can carry on the best battle in this game (...). There's no queen like humility for making the King surrender (C, 16/1–2).

God, by his passion, deliver us from dwelling on such words or thoughts as: "I have seniority," "I am older," "I have done much work," or "the other is treated better than I." If such thoughts come, they should be quickly cut off. If you dwell on this or begin to speak about them, the result is a pestilence from which great evils arise (C, 12/4).

With Teresa, we will not find a systematic explanation of ascetic practices, as we do with Saint John of the Cross who gives details of the active nights of feelings and the spirit. However, before giving her advice for prayer in *The Way of Perfection*, the Madre shows her daughters the climate in which union with God blossoms. Everything is explained in a loveable way and seems to be a hodge-podge, according to whatever comes to her mind. At times, we may be mistaken: the foundress is as exacting as the doctor of "nada." God knows only to give of himself, the King knows only to let himself be checkmated and put himself only into a heart where nothing is taken away from him.

Teresa who, as a small girl, envisioned herself as being beheaded by the Moors in order to conquer eternal happiness at the least cost, did not change her perspective. For her, the religious life was a call to give everything. The total gift of herself was only exacted after a longer lapse of time, but it still was equal to a true death. We have heard her say: "You came here to die for Christ."

We could perhaps be surprised at her insistence, which affirms her self-restriction to three points. It is true that she already spoke about poverty in *The Way of Perfection*. A few chapters later, when she spoke about prayer, she spoke about "a very resolute determination" and about perseverance. But, upon closer inspection, we observe that the three points mentioned here virtually cover the totality of the human experience. The love for one another, which she describes as a pure love, is a disinterested love and detached from what we would seek for ourselves. With reference to the renunciation of comforts, united with humility, they represent a detachment from one's self—a detachment for the body as well as for the soul. We must finally note that humility pre-empts all returns to one's self in a relationship with God. Teresian asceticism is, therefore, total and radical.

The different points highlighted in these chapters, of which we have only given a few excerpts, may perhaps present certain particularities which are due to the socio-cultural context of that era. The insistence regarding detachment with respect to one's parents and friends is easily understood in a very clerical society where each person feels that they have a say about the kind of boy or girl who enters into the religious life. In the same fashion, the special treatment accorded those of a certain social rank, the famous "pundonor," was a characteristic trait of Spain in the Golden Century. But this particular coloration did not stop the Madre from getting to the bottom of things. If the religious life consists of contesting the faults of a society in the name of the gospel, we could say that Teresa knew how to zero in on her objectives with precision.

She is a realist about that which refers to friendship relationships. The idealistic portrait that she outlines about spiritual love is, in fact, an ideal. She knew how to recognize that a little passion and a search for self could be mixed in at the beginning. But we also remember the very circumstantial principle she gave, in a small community of thirteen, or even twenty-one: that affection, even the purest kind, must not have the result of pairing people off, even less of making cliques. Everyone must be friends with no preferences shown. We will note the wisdom of this rule of conduct. It makes for a closed small society. What Teresa prescribed here, for the smooth running of her communities, she cultivated with other close friends, male or female. But she did this outside of the convent!

We can find, in chapters 4 to 16 of *The Way of Perfection*, a subject for a good examination of conscience; there, we also find suggestions or ideas for an orientation with the view of advancing oneself in the union with God. If the days spent in prayer in the company of Teresa must conclude with a resolution, the reading of these chapters would particularly be profitable.

However, some people find themselves becoming discouraged. As we said, Teresa is as radical as John of the Cross. The kingdom of God calls resolved people. At all times, we will perhaps be pleasantly surprised and encouraged to find assertions such as the following throughout the pages of these chapters:

> If we embrace the Creator and care not at all for the whole of creation, his Majesty will infuse the virtues. Doing what we can, little by little, we will hardly have anything else to fight against (C, 8/1).

Teresa knows what she is talking about: the first step on this path certainly gives "a very resolute determination." But when the Lord can gauge the seriousness of our resolution, he takes matters into his own hands in a way. In a way so that detachment, which is the preliminary condition for the union, becomes a resulting fruit of the union. Is this a vicious circle or an error in logic by our author? Not at all! But it is a vital circle, if we could call it that, which Teresa described, in her inimitable way:

It is a great thing to have experienced the friendship and favor he shows toward those who journey on this road and how he takes care of almost all the expenses (C, 23/5).

What are you waiting for, soul of so little faith, to decide to go on your voyage? Do you know how to respond to the invitation? Would it not be by making the prayer of the liturgy, inspired by the bride in the Song of Songs, your own: "Draw me to you, we follow the scent of your perfume"?

REFLECTION QUESTIONS

Do I pray that God will provide me with the graces of those few things I need to find joy and fulfillment in this life? Do I ask that I will be able to relate to others, to understand and love others, and to recognize the love for God within others? Do I recognize the need for detachment in my life? Do I understand that there are events and people that are beyond my control, and that faith and trust in God (rather than worry, anger, or frustration) is the grace that is needed at these times? Do I see the need for the grace of humility in my life? In what ways might humility help me to cope with those events and people that are beyond my control but in which I am deeply invested emotionally?

DAY NINE

Resolute Determination

FOCUS POINT

God is our focus. God is the reason we are alive, and it is toward God that we strive. We must be determined not to lose our focus. Prayer ensures that we will not. Prayer can help us keep our eyes on our goal—eternity with God in heaven. Every part of our life—our workaday world, our leisure time, our dealings with others—can be immersed in prayer, and our focus can be on God through all aspects of our life. We must attach our hearts to God, and let go of those lesser attachments that attempt to distract us from loving God and serving him in love.

Now returning to those who want to journey on this road and continue until they reach the end, which is to drink from this water of life, I say that how they begin is very important—in fact, all important. They must have a great and very resolute determination to persevere until reaching the end, come what may, happen what may, whatever work is involved, whatever criticism arises, whether they arrive or whether they die on the road, or even if they don't have the courage for the trials that are met, or if the whole world collapses (C, 21/2).

Consider our soul to be like a castle made entirely out of a diamond or of a very clear crystal, in which there are many rooms, just as in heaven there are many dwelling places (1D, 1/1).

Insofar as I can understand, the door of entry to this castle is prayer (1D, 1/7).

Perseverance is most necessary here. One always gains much through perseverance. But the attacks made by the devils in a thousand ways afflict the soul more in these rooms than in the previous ones (...). It is in this stage that the devils represent these snakes [worldly things] and the temporal pleasures of the present as though almost eternal. They bring to mind the esteem one has in the world, one's friends and relatives, one's health [when there are thoughts of penitential practices] (...) and a thousand other obstacles (2D, 1/3).

Certainly, the soul undergoes great trials here. If the devil, especially, realizes that it has all it needs in its temperament and habits to advance far (2D, 1/5).

What shall we say to those who, through perseverance and the mercy of God, have won these battles and have entered the rooms of the third stage, if not: Blessed is the man who fears the Lord? (...) I am certain the Lord never fails to give a person like this security of conscience (3D, 1/1).

In *The Interior Castle*, Teresa marks out the road for us that she has traveled. But she did it in such a way that each of us could find our own path. That fact is true, even if, in the highest rooms, what she teaches remains totally appropriate for those who have not yet advanced that far. Just as she already did in *The Way of Perfection*, she exhorts us to commit ourselves to this way of seeking the union with God.

For her, this way is the way of prayer. The adventure with God is conceived by her as a progressive interiorization. The soul is a castle made of crystal in which there are many dwelling places, which are more and more central. At its very depth lives the King, who promised to come to us and make his dwelling place there (see Jn 14:23). But the devil invites us to live at the surface of ourselves, that is to say, on the exterior of this castle. "For where your treasure is, there your heart will be also" (Mt 6: 21). The realities of the world, necessary, useful, or superfluous, when they are not a nuisance, solicit our covetous desires. Our hearts become attached to them and, all at once, we live for them. Let us question ourselves about the importance that a certain affection has in our lives. Yet, according to Teresa, the Christian life is an attempt to give the interior guest all of the space: God said to Abraham, "walk before me" (Gen 17: 1). The soul is thus invited to progressively penetrate to the interior of itself until it permanently dwells—if God allows it—with the Guest who dwells in the Seven Dwelling Places.

Prayer is the prescribed way, the door to the Castle. But Teresa does not make a distinction between prayer and a life of prayer. The business of friendship, as we have said, develops as much among the pots and pans as in the "nooks." It remains that this mutual and very intimate presence finds its strongest expression in prayer, which is the door to the Castle.

Teresa fought her entire life for the right of the simple faithful person to have a life of prayer. She wasn't afraid to confront the raised eyebrows of the experts of her time, who feared for the deviations of the lesser educated people, and even more, for those of women. For Teresa, her fight for prayer, even in its highest forms if God wanted to accord it to them, was nothing other than proclaiming the rights of all baptized people to the integral development of a life of grace.

For her battle, we must not haggle over the means. We recognize all of the energy that Teresa put into her "resolute determination" to undertake the way of perfection. We must persevere in this way of prayer. We must start again when our energy wanes. We must remain faithful when, the first wave of satisfaction having faltered, we find ourselves distracted, empty, and with the feeling that we have wasted our time. It is at that moment we undoubtedly strongly sense, not the prohibitions of the "experts" of Teresa's time, but what the current popular slogans say about the demobilizing role of prayer, about denouncing it as being a flight from reality. The Madre rebuffed the objections of her times. In our times, we could make a corresponding litany. The advice of an experienced spiritual companion could then become necessary to help to bring about discernment and keep us focused on the goal. We must remember that the prince of shadows disguises himself as an angel of light and presents temptation under the guise of goodness. Teresa remembered that, in her youth, she had the idea of abandoning prayer *under the cover of humility.*

The spirit of evil hounds so much that, when we are on this route, we do not ever travel alone. A soul that lifts itself up lifts up the world. Some are called to bring along many others, and the tempter reserves his most terrible attacks for them. The Second Dwelling Place rapidly explains spiritual combat. There, Teresa, the daughter and sister of military men, uses warlike vocabulary with which she is familiar. We can't reproach her for having sweetened her presentation. The pages in which she speaks to us correspond to those from John of the Cross' *Ascent of Mount Carmel.* Teresa never lacks giving us the necessary encouragement.

She also shows us that these efforts, more or less prolonged, will bring results. In the Third Dwelling Place, Teresa describes the soul that has succeeded in acquiring good habits through the strength of perseverance. Prayer is no longer put into question; it has become simpler, more charged with love than consolation. Life itself has become virtuous, where deliberate— serious or venial—sins are not to be feared, and good habits are acquired. The soul could give thanks for having reached that point, for "Blessed are those who fear the Lord."

However, the person's efforts have only just begun. These efforts, undoubtedly orchestrated by the grace of God, still remain human efforts. It has all the human characteristics, it is limited and sporadic. And then if a great trial blows in—Teresa gives a few examples of these—the beautiful building that was painfully built will reveal its fragility. What then is it lacking?

May the Lord take matters in to his own hands. Here, the friendly comparison also used by Thérèse of Lisieux enlightens us. A child is at the bottom of the stairs; he is too small to climb to the first step and he wants to join his mother who is at the top. Thérèse said, he lifts his little foot to try to go up. But he is too small and his gesture is inadequate. If he quickly abandons the attempt, his mother will think that he is fine at the bottom and will leave him there. But if he continues to try to make the attempt, the mother will understand and she will take the initiative. She will go down, pick him up in her arms, and take him up the stairs.

Lord, you only wait for a gesture from us of perseverance. If we know how to address you, the time will come when you will take matters into your own hands. That will be when you judge it to be right: whether it is in the first or the eleventh hour, it is your secret. But you will come. And we will no longer function in our human way, but in your way. Whether it is in prayer or in our daily lives, our activities will carry your mark. Thérèse of Lisieux spoke of stairs that we climbed in the arms of our mother. The Madre speaks of the water of contemplation. The comparisons are not important as long as they are understood! Lord, give me this water! And for that, give me the necessary determination to make you understand that, truly, I want it!

REFLECTION QUESTIONS

How do I deal with temptations in my life? Do I possess the resolute determination to reject the false promises and sugar-coated lies that temptation offers? How can I become more resolute, more determined, in my focus to serve and follow God? What people might I seek out to and be with who might strengthen my resolve and determination to serve God in love? What spiritual reading might benefit me in this regard? What strategies of contemplation and meditation might benefit me when temptations arise?

DAY TEN

The Two Troughs

FOCUS POINT

Jesus Christ is the "living water," which if we drink we will never thirst again. There is a wellspring in each of us. The water of this wellspring is living water, now that Jesus has united God and humankind by his sacrifice on the cross. By this act of sacrifice, humankind is saved, and the wellspring within each of us provides the necessary graces to proceed through our daily life. Empty promises of other waters that save—waters provided by someone besides God—need not concern us, and we should not be thirsty for such waters. The "living water" of God, the wellspring within us, satisfies and nourishes and cleanses us eternally.

I think I have already explained the nature of consolations in the spiritual life (...). The experiences that I call spiritual delight in God, that I termed the "prayer of quiet" elsewhere, are of a very different kind (...). Let's consider, for a better understanding, that we see two founts with water troughs. (For I don't find anything more appropriate to explain some spiritual experiences than water) (...).

These two troughs are filled with water in different ways; with one, the water comes from far away, artificially through many aqueducts and the use of much ingenuity; with the other, the source of the water is right there, and the trough fills without any noise. If the spring is abundant, as is this one we are speaking about, the water overflows once the trough is filled, forming a large stream. There is no need for any artificial skill, nor does the building of aqueducts have to continue; but water is always flowing from the spring.

The water coming from the aqueducts is comparable, in my opinion, to the consolations I mentioned that are drawn from meditation (...).

With the other trough, the water comes from its own source, which is God. And since his Majesty desires to do so—when he is pleased to grant some supernatural favor—he produces this delight with the greatest peace and quiet and sweetness in the very interior part of ourselves (4D, 2/ 1–4).

Well now, in speaking about what I said, I'd mention here, concerning the difference in prayer between consolations and spiritual delights, the term "consolations," I think, can be given to those experiences we ourselves acquire through our own meditation and petitions to the Lord, those that proceed from our own nature—although God does have a hand in them (...), but the consolations arise from the virtuous work itself that we perform, and it seems that we have earned them through our own effort and are rightly consoled for having engaged in such deeds. But if we reflect upon this, we see that we experience the same joyful consolations in many of the things that can happen to us on earth; for example: when somebody inherits a great fortune; (...) or when you see your husband or brother alive after someone has told you he is dead (4D, 1/4).

Spiritual delights begin in God, but human nature feels and enjoys them as much as it does those I mentioned [before] (...). Now I remember a line that we say at Prime, in the latter part of the verse at the end of the last psalm: Cum dilatasti cor meum ("When the heart was expanded") (4D, 1/4–5).

I was thinking, while writing this, about the line mentioned above: "Dilatasti cor meum," which means the heart was expanded. I don't think the experience is something that arises from the heart, but from another part, even more interior, as if from something deeper. I think this must be the center of the soul (...) (4D, 2/5).

At this point, we are at the stage where, as we have said before, the Holy Spirit himself takes things into his own hands. It is a transformation in our way of praying, acting, and living.

Understand this well, that when we are seriously determined to enter the ways of prayer, we have "undertaken" a certain procedure and, if we steer it toward the Lord and his glory—and with the concurrence of grace—we nevertheless continue to handle it humanly, as we handle everything else.

We will determine a certain regimen of prayer and sacramental life; we will examine its weak points; and we will assure ourselves of having spiritual accompaniment. We will advance through trial and error, keeping what gives us good results, experiencing consolations for proven successes. All of that is fine and good, and it could not be otherwise until God himself intervenes in a different way. But, finally, all of these efforts "functions," we could say, in the way of man, in no way more or less than in any other enterprise.

In the meantime, if it pleases God, he will introduce us to supernatural contemplation and, this time, he will make us pray and act in his own way, or at least in a way that carries his mark on it. Things will proceed differently. Saint John of the Cross described the effects of this adaptation as a type of void that the soul feels in prayer. It is the "night without feeling," of which he gives the signs, after having explained its necessity.

According to Teresa, she knew only how to give witness to things that had happened to her. And that is why she describes certain effects that the soul feels and that bear the mark of the divine manner, according to which, we could say, the human being works.

She speaks to us then about these "gustos," these joys which God procures for us and which come from the deepest part of the being "which end up flooding everything." Everyone has his own way of saying it: it is rather intriguing to state what Saint Ignatius speaks rather enigmatically about in two lines of Rule 330 as the "consolation without a cause." In contrast, Teresa takes many pages to develop as the comparison between two troughs! She will also describe the prayer of quiet and this variation which we call prayer of supernatural retreat.

Don't be disconcerted by these descriptions of the primary

favors being called "supernatural." It is true that they are beyond human effort and that there is no recipe to attain them,
but they do make up the experience of many Christians,
whether they are established in habitual fervor or whether God
prepares them only for conversion. Many people could give
witness that, during the course of a retreat, for example, they
had been filled with the joy of knowing that they are loved by
God in spite of their misery. That consciousness has taken hold
of them suddenly, without any apparent cause, and has left
them appeased, confident, and feeling generous. Others have
known times of prayer during which they found themselves
gently turned toward God, with no effort on their part, "eyes
turned towards the interior guest, knowing about nothing except this presence." Happy with this experience and naively
confident, they have perhaps said to themselves that they finally know how to pray. This is a serious error! During the
next meeting, they find themselves with their habitual problems.

This "state of grace" had been given to us freely. These are
the first approaches of a God who wants to transform his part-
ners and bring them to the business of friendship which is situated, we could say, at his own level. The relationship with the
Lord always happens through faith, but it has a divine taste of
sorts. We have been given an indication of "seeing how good
the Lord is" by experiencing, in our psyches, "a way" that is
not our own, but his.

In the Fourth Dwelling Place, Teresa speaks of the prayer
of quiet and of her "gustos." Perhaps it is permitted to stretch
her teaching to other experiences of the same type which happen either in prayer or in the thousands of experiences of daily
life. Undoubtedly, this is the point at which to cite these verses
of Scripture that are read often, these details of an evangelical

scene, which are very familiar, but which, at this time, take on a new meaning and extraordinary flavor. Everything happens as if we have discovered it for the first time and as if it has been personally destined for us. We know that we will never forget these events and that they will, from now on, form a part of our spiritual personality. They also, like the forms of prayer that Saint Teresa described, will bring us enlightenment and the fruit of the Holy Spirit: joy, peace, generosity, confidence in others, and self-control (see Gal 5:22).

We have only cited the graces of a loving knowledge of God for an instant. There are others which stem even more from the domain of action. Saint Vincent de Paul was not familiar, as he said, with these forms of supernatural prayer. Nevertheless, the spark that pushed him to take the shackles of a galley-slave are really the same, in a practical sense, as a prayer of supernatural introspection! It is the divine way which appeared there as well. We could say as much about the important and courageous decisions taken in peace, and of which the subject perceived, at the same time, that they were his own, but which, however, came from something that was deeper than he; or an enlightened prudence that makes one see clearly and gives one a secure orientation in a complicated endeavor. When we remind ourselves about these experiences—after the fact, for it would be dangerous to believe that we are connected directly to the Holy Spirit—we cannot stop ourselves from thinking that there, again, some favors have been granted freely to us. This time, they stem from what the theologian could have called the gift of strength or the gift of counsel. But they are manifestations of this divine enterprise—manifestations of the enterprise of which the Lord is the master, and which he grants when he wants to, in favor of those he chooses, and according to the modalities he chooses.

Teresa said: "Lord, give me this water." Again, a limited, sporadic gift, but such a precious one! The form that it takes is not holiness itself. Lord, if you give it, it is for the use of your servants; for their conversion, for their progress, or for the mission in which they are involved. As Teresa said, you could choose to give nothing of yourself in this world, to fulfill your friend when he will join you in the other. But I also know that you have no greater desire than to give of yourself, to give us a taste of you; and that if "your delights are to be with the children of man," you want these delights to be shared with your friend.

Then, Lord, if it is your wish, "give me some of this water," the effusion of your Holy Spirit, or at least a few drops. For, "I will run the way of your commandments, for you enlarge my heart [understanding]" (see Ps 119:32). And when I will know to recognize your passages in my life, I will have even more thirst and will want to see the trickle of water become a torrent.

REFLECTION QUESTIONS

Am I aware of the "living water" that wells up within me as a result of Jesus Christ's saving act? Am I filled with joy when God's graces well up within me, moving my friendship with God to newer and deeper levels of loving communication? How do I respond to offers of other "saving waters"? Can I pray for the grace to be better in touch with the wellspring inside of me? How do I respond during those periods when I feel as though my wellspring has dried up? How might the company of others benefit me during those periods?

DAY ELEVEN

The Silkworm

FOCUS POINT

There is a transformation that occurs when our will finally submits to that of our heavenly Father. This transformation is so dramatic, so powerful, that the person we were before bears little to no resemblance to the person we become. Like a worm that becomes a butterfly (as Saint Teresa puts it), we transform from the mundane, the ugly, into the extraordinary, the beautiful. We are perfected in love by our actions, by repeating actions of love until they are performed as an automatic response to the need we see—the need for love and service.

You must have already heard about his marvels manifested in the way silk originates, for only he could have invented something like that. The silkworms come from seeds about the size of little grains of pepper (...). When the warm weather comes, and the leaves begin to appear on the mulberry trees, the seeds start to live, for they are dead until then. The worms nourish themselves on mulberry leaves until, having grown to full size, they settle on some twigs. There, with their mouths, they go about spinning the silk and making very thick little cocoons in which they enclose themselves. The silkworm, which is fat and ugly, then dies, and a little white butterfly, which is very pretty, comes forth from the cocoon (5D, 2/2).

Well, once this silkworm is grown (...), it begins to spin the silk and build the house wherein it will die. I would like to point out here that this house is Christ. Somewhere, it seems to me, I have read or heard that our life is hidden in Christ or in God (both are the same), or that our life is Christ (5D, 2/4).

Therefore, get to work, my daughters! Let's be quick to weave this little cocoon by ridding ourselves of our self-love and self-will, our attachment to any earthly thing, and by performing deeds of penance, prayer, mortification, obedience, and of all the other things you already know you must do (...). Let it die; let this silkworm die, just as it does in completing what it was created to do! And you will see how we see God, as well as ourselves placed inside his greatness, just like this little silk-worm is inside its cocoon. Keep in mind that I say "see God," that is the way he shows his presence in this kind of union (5D, 2/6).

Oh, greatness of God! How transformed the soul is when it comes out of this prayer after having been placed within the greatness of God and so closely joined with him (...). Truly, I tell you that the soul doesn't recognize itself. Look at the dif-

ference there is between an ugly worm and a little white butterfly; it is the same for the soul. The soul doesn't know how it could have merited so much good (5D, 2/7).

The parables of the silkworm, the chess game, the two troughs, and the castle are among the most celebrated in Teresa's works. This one warns us that prayer, as she wrote in these passages, is a rare favor. When the "gustos" of infused contemplation, the subject of the Fourth Dwelling Place, are experienced as relatively common, we find ourselves faced with a form of prayer, the prayer of union, which consists of the soul plunging itself into God. Its activities are suspended for a period of time and it loses, by the very act itself, the notion of itself, its environment, and a sense of time. Briefly, the prayer of union is, of itself, ecstatic, even if it doesn't seem as such at times. We understand that the beneficiary of it has the impression of being immersed in an abyss from which it emerges regenerated.

However, Teresa was careful to indicate that this kind of death, controlled by God, is situated in mortification, to which all Christians are called: the renunciation of one's self and one's self-will in order to welcome the love of God. This is a statement of great importance, as we shall see later.

Let us also note that after having described this form of prayer, Teresa, above all, insisted on the effects that it brought with it. The soul couldn't recognize itself. It was like the butterfly with respect to the silkworm: since it was made to fly in God's world, it doesn't know where to light here on earth, for nothing satisfies it here. From that time on, its world is God's world. Teresa, deprived of the Bible and having learned of the gospels only through the liturgical offices or through quotations in other sources, remembers, without knowing that she was citing Saint Paul, having heard that our life is hidden in God or, for us, our life is Christ. From that time on, she knew that she was capable of anything, for it is Christ who gives her strength. This prayer of union is the one which makes dazzling holiness, that of the apostles, Francis Xavier and the Curé of Ars, the one that gives strength to the martyrs, wisdom to the Doctors, and humility to the virgins.

However, we must ask a question of our spirit. For ordinary Christians, what interest do they have in these lofty favors? Is it not presumptuous to desire them? But to say that they do not concern us, would that not be rushing things a bit? For God does not grant his favors without a reason.

This is where Teresa's answer is ingenious. This prayer of union, which is ecstatic, of which she had been a beneficiary for a long time, in her eyes, is only a privileged means to reach the goal, a "short cut," as she called it. Let us hear what she said:

> Since so much gain comes from entering this place, it will be good to avoid giving the impression that those to whom the Lord doesn't give things that are so supernatural are left without hope. True union can very well be reached, with God's help, if we make the effort to obtain it by keeping our wills fixed only on that which is God's will (5D, 3/3).

Further on, she adds:

> This union with God's will is the union I have desired all my life; it is the union I ask the Lord for always and the one that is clearest and safest (5D, 3/5).

Understand what this union takes. Christian perfection, Teresa repeated it in every possible way, does not consist of thinking a great deal, but in loving a great deal. We all know this anecdote that is a part of Saint Aloysius of Gonzaga's "fioretti," or little sayings. Speaking with two friends about the question of knowing what they would do if they were going to prepare to appear before God in a short while: one said he would go to confession; the other, that he would go to the chapel. The saint answered: "Oh, well, I would continue to play ball, since that is what the Lord asked to me to do right now!" To adhere to God's will at all times is to accept the situation in which we are at present with love, and through it, reflect the Law and the prophets! That is the union that Teresa desired and sought her entire life.

Undoubtedly, it is difficult to adhere constantly to the Lord's will. We accomplish it, then we fail. It may take more than a lifetime to achieve it. May we be found, in our final hours, in a state of total and complete giving. That is the common hope. The Lord always grants this prayer of union to whomever he wishes. This union, by means of an extraordinary shortcut, leads to a permanent union of will. But this shortcut is not holiness. It is a way of access, mainly given to those who God destines for an exceptional mission in the Church.

Hence this interest in Teresa's teachings. The description of the effects of the prayer of union should not arouse our jealousy, but rather enflame our love and make us more generous in the way of the commandments.

As the psalm says: "The Lord is my portion, I promise to keep your words" (Ps 119:57). It is with this perspective that we make the following words of your saint Teresa our own, Lord:

The Lord asks of us only two things: love of his Majesty and love of our neighbor. These are what we must work for (...). The most certain sign, in my opinion, as to whether or not we are observing these two laws is whether we observe well the love of neighbor (...). And be certain that the more advanced you see you are in the love for your neighbor, the more advanced you will be in the love of God, for the love his Majesty has for us is so great that to repay us for our love of neighbor, he will, in a thousand ways, increase the love we have for him. I cannot doubt this (5D, 3/7–8).

Lord, may we no longer doubt you, or ourselves!

REFLECTION QUESTIONS

In what ways am I transformed during prayer? In what ways do I strive for perfection in love? Do I give myself away in love for others and for God? Do I give myself away in love with such frequency and ease that I actually think very little about the fact that I am pleasing God with my loving service? When I look back at moments of loving service, am I aware of times when I experienced a "union of will" with God, that is, when the will of God and my own will were so "in sync" that I was unable to tell where my will left off and God's began?

DAY TWELVE

Martha and Mary Magdalene

FOCUS POINT

There is a balance we must seek in our relationship with the Lord. We must be content with both sides of love: an active love, in which we serve our God; and a more passive love, in which we sit at our Lord's feet, listening to him speak and enjoying his presence. There is a joy in this balance. Our love for God can only be tested by going out into our daily lives and working in love for God with others. Yet, our goal must always be God, to be in his presence, so that our daily lives are not lived in pride—for our personal glory—but rather to glorify the holy name of God.

Believe me, Martha and Mary Magdalene must join together in order to show hospitality to the Lord, and have him always present and not host him badly by failing to give him something to eat. How would Mary Magdalene, always seated at his feet, provide him with food, if her sister didn't help her? His food is that we bring souls to him, using every means possible, so that they may be saved and praise him always.

You will make two objections: one, that he said that Mary Magdalene had chosen the better part. The answer is that she had already performed Martha's task, pleasing the Lord by washing his feet and drying them with her hair. Do you think it would be a small mortification for a woman of nobility like her to wander through the streets (…) and enter a house she had never entered before and afterwards, suffer the criticism of the Pharisee and the many other things she must have suffered? The people saw a woman like her change so much— and, as we know, she was among such malicious people—and they saw her friendship with the Lord, whom they vehemently abhorred, and saw that she acted like a saint (…). All of that was enough to cause them to comment on the life she had formerly lived. If, nowadays, there is so much gossip against persons who are not as notorious, what must have been said then? I tell you, Sisters, the better part came after many trials and much mortification, for even if there were no other trial than to see his Majesty abhorred, that would be an intolerable one (…). I believe, the many trials afterwards that she suffered upon the death of the Lord, and in the years that she subsequently lived in his absence, must have been terrible torment. You see, she wasn't always in the delight of contemplation at the feet of the Lord (7D, 4/12–13).

The preceding passage that the Madre has written about the life of Mary Magdalene was a personal one. First, she had not had the benefit of modern exegetical education, and the character of Mary Magdalene was the one presented in the Liturgy, that is to say, both the sinner, Mary of Bethany, the sister of Martha and Lazarus, and Mary of Magdalene. This problem remains of little importance for the spiritual life. "*Lex orandi, lex credendi,*" the liturgy is the mistress of faith and prayer. Finally and even more, Mary Magdalene was Teresa herself. Mary Magdalene was her ideal and her model. A woman, having fully assumed her femininity, with joy, we could say, Teresa saw herself in Mary Magdalene's attitudes and gestures, by going to the Lord with her entire being, including her feelings. The love of her model was not exempt, we might say, from a suspicion of jealousy, until the day she heard the Lord say to her: "She had been my friend during my days on earth. You take her place now" (FVD, July 22, 1572).

Teresa, conscious of her misery, found herself totally in the sinner, begging for forgiveness. But the contemplative, thirsting for the message, had no trouble seeing that the best part was to have been seated at the feet of the Master, listening to his words. She had no contempt at all for Martha—the texts are sufficient to show this—to the point that she justified Mary Magdalene by showing that she had first done Martha's tasks. Teresa had become Mary Magdalene to such an extent that we see her explaining her itinerary, starting from the difficulties she had experienced herself. The Pharisees and Mary Magdalene's compatriots had never, without a doubt, said of her: "she acted like a saint." But we know in return that this had been said of Teresa of Ávila, at a time when her mystical experiences were common knowledge.

The most decisive evangelical event for Teresa was the

marvelous meeting in the garden on Easter morning (see Jn 20:11–18). In effect, Mary Magdalene was the one who heard herself being told: "Do not hold onto me...but go tell my brothers." It doesn't seem that one advances much by affirming that this scene exerted a strong influence on our saint in the two or three years (1569–1572) that preceded her entry into the Seven Dwelling Places and the grace of her spiritual marriage. In 1571, she noted:

> The vivid desire that was so impetuous that I had to die, has left me, in particular, since the feast of Mary Magdalene when I decided to live with all my heart to serve God; the desire to see him always comes back and, in spite of my efforts, it is impossible to push this out of my mind (FVD, 1571).

This desire left her, or at least lessened definitively after the grace of November 18, 1572, when she was made the bride of the Lord, and when she heard herself being told: "Nothing could separate her from him, Jesus" (see Rom 8:35), and that she must now take care of the Lord's business, and that he, Jesus, would take care of hers (7D, 2/1).

Like Mary Magdalene, then, Teresa heard the call: "Do not hold onto me...but go tell my brothers." Go proclaim the joy of Easter, at the risk of being contradicted. The apostles said that it was "an idle tale" (Lk 24: 11) when they heard it from the holy women. Teresa also knew contradiction and battles. They reached a culminating point for Teresa in the years 1575–1580. This sister of conquistadors was ready for the battle. She gave herself, without a second thought, to the work of the Lord.

The ten years that remained in her life after the grace of November 1572, would be, it was said, years of intense activity. She would be Martha through her work, but she never stopped being Mary Magdalene at the same time. No task could turn her away from the company of the interior Guest. No illness either: her body ached all over and she vomited every night. But suffering did not take hold of her. Neither does any other affection: totally given to everyone, by writing letters every night until 2:00 A.M., she could, in her correspondence with Father Gratien or Mary of Saint Joseph, give free reign to the tenderness of a heart that belongs only to Jesus, her Lord and Master. The harshest controversies about the reform of the order did not change her concentration: *The Interior Castle*, written at perhaps the most dramatic moment of her existence, breathes only of peace and serenity.

At the same time, this same work gave witness to the degree of tempered rigidity which her doctrine had reached. She understood that the summit of the union with God did not consist of arranging a tranquil solitude for herself, as busy as she was with thoughts of the Lord, but of her acceptance of being led, if that was the case, "there, where we don't want to go." She wrote:

> Here, my daughters, is where love must be seen: not hiding in corners, but in the midst of things. And believe me, that even though there may be more failings, and even some slight losses, our gain will be incomparably greater. Note that I am always presupposing that these things are done out of obedience and charity. For if these are not a factor, I always feel that solitude is better (...).
>
> (...) For people who are always enclosed in solitude, however holy they may be in their own opinion, do not know whether they are patient or humble, nor

do they have the means of knowing this. How could it be known whether a man were valiant, if he were not seen in battle? (F, 5/15).

Lord, at times, I have also undoubtedly desired to take on the role of Mary Magdalene. My intention was appropriate, yet perhaps not exempt from an unwarranted desire to be free from all worry and trouble. Help me to want only what you want and, in all cases, to unite Mary Magdalene and Martha to my poor self.

> *Give me wealth or want,*
> *Delight or distress, (...)*
> *If You want me to rest,*
> *I desire it for love;*
> *If to labor,*
> *I will die working:*
> *Sweet Love say*
> *Where, how, and when.*
> *What do you want of me?*
> *(Po 2).*

REFLECTION QUESTIONS

In what ways am I like Mary? In what ways am I like Martha? Do I prefer Mary's way of adoration to Martha's way of service or vice versa? Which area—adoration or service—do I neglect in favor of the other? What can I do to remedy this? Do I seek new ways of adoration in my life of worship? Do I seek new challenges in my daily life that bear witness to my love for God? Who might I seek out to help me address these concerns?

DAY THIRTEEN

Harm Done to the Kingdom of France

FOCUS POINT

There is an innate desire in us all to experience and promote unity among one another. While this is rarely possible, be it in politics or religion or whatever else we hold dear, there is always the hope that common ground will be reached, that those who do not understand the whole truth will experience a revelation and join those already living that reality. What can one person do to assist this unity? Teresa addresses this very concern below, since this was an important issue facing herself, her community, and her Church at that point in world history.

At that time, news reached me of the harm being done in France, and of the havoc the Lutherans had caused and how much this...sect was growing. The news distressed me greatly, and, as though I could do something or were someone important, I cried to the Lord and begged him that I might help remedy so much confusion. I felt able to give my life a thousand times just to save one of the many souls that were being lost there (...). As a result, I resolved to do the little that was within my power to do; that is, to follow the evangelical counsels as perfectly as I could and strive to get these few persons who live here to do the same (C, 1/2).

Four years later, or, a little more than that, a Franciscan friar happened to come to see me. His name was Friar Alonso Maldonado, a great servant of God; he had the same desires for the good of souls as I, but he was able to transfer them into deeds, for which I greatly envied him. He had recently come back from the Indies. He began to tell me about the millions of souls that were being lost there for want of Christian instruction, and before leaving, he gave us a sermon, and, through his words, encouraged us to do penance. He then left. I was so grief-stricken over the loss of so many souls that I couldn't contain myself. I went to a hermitage in tears. I cried out to the Lord, begging him to give me the means to be able to win some souls through my prayers, since the devil was carrying away so many, and I wasn't able to do anything else (F, 1/7).

The world is all in flames (...). This is not the time to be discussing matters that have little importance to God (C, 1/5).

Human means are not sufficient to stop the spread of this fire (...). It seemed to me that what is necessary is a different ap-

proach, the approach of a lord when, in times of war, his land is overrun with enemies and he finds himself restricted on all sides. He withdraws to a city that he has fortified well and from where, sometimes, he was able to strike at his foe. Those who are in the city, being chosen people, can do more by themselves than many cowardly soldiers can (…).

But why have I said this? So that you understand, my Sisters, that what we must ask God is that, in this little castle, where there are already good Christians, not one of us will go over to the enemy, and that God will make the captains of this castle, or city [the preachers and theologians], very advanced in the way of the Lord (…) that they advance very far in the perfection of religious life and their vocation (…) (C, 3/1–2).

T eresa was "a daughter of the Church." All that she had, in her family, her parish, her order, or the spiritual currents of her time, she had received from the Church. She suffered *for* the Church, but also, as did all of the saints, *at the hand of* the Church, as she was put in the middle by the authorities who acted in opposite ways. How could she disassociate herself from the Church and her life in this world?

Some of her contemporaries questioned her, at times, about her ecumenism. It is an anachronistic question. A contemporary of the great schism of the Reformation, she prayed with all of her strength so that the rupture would not happen, the time having not yet come to try to approach the separated segments. However, in this way, she was a precursor of Vatican II; she let it be known that religious decisions come from the conscience and that we do not convert heretics by force.

The apostolic worry, which never failed her, crystallized

itself for her through two circumstances. First, she was made
aware of the situation in France, which was torn apart by religious wars. A neighboring country, and an enemy most of the
time, France was no less a bastion of Christianity. King Philip II,
anxious to avoid the extension of the fires which burned on
the other side of the Pyrenees, ordered all of the religious of
Spain to pray, and hold processions and various demonstra-
tions of devotion for this intention. Moreover, Teresa had
friends, who were theologians, who had acted as consultants
for the Council of Trent. The harm that was being done to
France was discussed there, notably by a reluctant interven-
tion on the part of the cardinal of Lorraine, on Christmas Eve,
1561. On the other hand, she reports to us about Friar
Maldonado's visit, and his return from the Americas. Teresa,
judging others based on her own values, thought that the conquistadors went there as propagators of the faith. She was close
to considering her childhood companion, her brother Rodrigo,
a martyr, as he died in combat on the shores of the Rio de la
Plata. She fell hard from her lofty thoughts when she heard
Friar Maldonado's vehement reports.

What could one do in Spain in the sixteenth century, when
one was a woman religious and the Church did not want to
recognize monastic orders other than those that were cloistered? We heard it from her: she and her sisters would be "pur-
veyors of munitions" for the fighters who were the priests,
theologians, and preachers of the gospel.

These reported events would give the Teresian Carmelites
a decisive orientation. Teresa of the Child Jesus, by affirming
that she went to Carmel to pray for the intentions of the priests,
only repeated a fundamental intuition of her Mother Foundress.
We could make an interesting comment about this subject. If
we could compare the Constitution written by Teresa of Ávila

to that of the Blessed Frances of Amboise, the Foundress, a century before the first Carmelite convents in Brittany, we find that their dispositions are generally the same. Moreover, putting the insistence on prayer aside, these are what we find in the majority of convents of the time. However, the spirit differs by the accents which are clear-cut: by simplifying it a little, let us say that one enters the Teresian Carmel in order to take part, an essential part, in the mission of the Church: service through prayer, or more precisely, through love. It is again Thérèse of Lisieux who sums up this orientation the best: "My Mother, in the heart of the Church, I will be love, thus, I will be everything" (Letter to Sister Mary of the Sacred Heart).

If this teaching, in fact, is essential to Carmel, it is also of capital importance to the Church. The mission could not do without the commitment of man. It is necessary for the missionaries to leave their country and cross the sea; the Doctors must teach; the pastors must work their fingers to the bone; even going as far as giving blood witness when it is requested. Also, the workers for the kingdom cannot work without a minimum of methodology (we think of the Jesuits in China a little after the death of Teresa or of the "reductions" in Paraguay); without certain techniques, without an "apostolic guideline" in which we determine, in concert and in faithfulness with the directives of the pastors; or without a minimum of material (think of Saint Maximilian Kolbe's print shops). But we also know that "unless the Lord builds the house; those who build it labor in vain" (Ps 127:1).

The role of the contemplatives is to be the "keepers of the lighthouse," who keep watch over the fire, so that each person could navigate in safety, even in fog and bad weather. But even more as the keepers of the lighthouse, the contemplatives, by their presence, are a reminder: that we should be careful not to forget that no navigation is possible if the vigil isn't assured on the shore. In other words, a relationship with the Lord through prayer is indispensable for each of us, no matter what stage of life we are at, and in all circumstances. Only the modalities change. It is a question of nuance, not of the base.

Lord, so that the redemption that you brought to the world is effective, we need a "receptive pole." It is necessary for men and women to be there, like the Blessed Virgin Mary at Cana, to present the problems of humans; and, above all, as she was at Calvary, to welcome, in the name of the world, the blood that flowed from above on the cross. That is why you never cease to call men and women to devote their lives to prayer.

But there is no such thing as one "monk's prayer" which is different from the others' prayers. It is as if the monks were marginalized, each devoted to a task, certainly respectable, but separate. And there is no longer one apostolate from which the cloistered orders could disassociate themselves under the pretext that they are devoted to prayer. Prayer would then have a demobilizing role. Teresa repeated it to us enough: true prayer does not consist of thinking a great deal, but loving a great deal! Then it is necessary to deliver one's heart and freedom in order to agree to everything that you want. That is why the person who truly prays sees, in all apostles, a brother devoted to the powerful task which calls them to give of their whole beings. That is why the apostle sees, in the person who prays, a brother, a sister, who is called to leave everything—and it is necessary to leave everything!—in order to also be completely available to whatever you desire and totally receptive to the gift you give them, Lord. It is a gift that you offer to the whole world, which they must transmit to all humanity, in the same way as a receptive pole welcomes the current.

REFLECTION QUESTIONS

In what ways do I promote ecumenical dialogue in my community? If I do not now, in what manner might I best serve God and his Church in the conversion of others to the Catholic faith? Is there a group currently in my church—such as the Legion of Mary—that I might considering becoming a part of? If I do not already, can I take time in my daily prayers to pray for the conversion of all sinners and for the unity of the Christian churches of the world? What documents or books might I consider reading in order to get a better grasp on the Church's understanding and goals for dialogue between Christian denominations?

DAY FOURTEEN

The Lord Walks Among the Pots and Pans

FOCUS POINT

Jesus came to us and lived with us as a poor man. He spent his time with poor, uneducated people, many of whom were ill. He loved and served these people, sharing with them all that he had. As Teresa was called to serve in this manner, so are we all called by Christ. Adoration and service. Mary and Martha. The monstrance and the "least of my brothers and sisters": we are called to seek Christ in all of these, because he is indeed in each one, waiting for us to engage him. We must leave no facet of our lives unturned toward Jesus.

The soul's progress does not lie in thinking a great deal but in loving a great deal.

How does one acquire this love? By being determined to work and to suffer, and by applying this principle at all times (...).

When either of these two things (the tasks of obedience and help for our neighbor) presents itself, time is demanded, and also the abandonment of what we so much desire to give God, which, in our opinion, is to be alone, thinking of him and delighting in the delights that he gives us. But to put aside these delights for either of these other two things is to give delight to him and do the work for him, as he, himself, said: "What you did for one of these little ones, you did for me." And in matters touching on obedience, he doesn't want the soul who truly loves him to take any other path than the one he did: "obediens usque ad mortem."

If this is true, from where does the displeasure come which, for the most part, is felt when one has not spent a large part of the day withdrawn and absorbed in God, even though we are busy with other useful things? In my opinion, there are two reasons for this displeasure: the first and primary one is the very subtle self-love that is mixed in here. This self-love does not allow one to understand how much we prefer pleasing ourselves rather than God. For, clearly, after a soul begins to taste how sweet the Lord is, it is more pleasing for the body to be resting without work and for the soul to be receiving delight.

O charity of those who truly love the Lord and know their own nature! How little rest they can have if they see they may play a small part in getting even one soul to make progress and love God more, or consoling it, or by taking away some danger from it. How poorly it would then rest if it rests alone!

(...). It would be a distressing thing if God were clearly telling us to go after something that matters to him and we would not want to do so, but want to remain looking at him because that is more pleasing to us!

(...) Well, come now, my daughters, don't be sad when obedience draws you to involvement in exterior matters. Know that if it is in the kitchen, the Lord walks among the pots and pan helping you both interiorly and exteriorly (F, 5/2–5, 8).

"The Lord walks among the pots and pans." This is a celebrated saying of Teresa's and is indicative of the style of our author. Did we notice that she echoes the last scene in the Gospel of Saint John in which the Lord "manifests his presence" (that is the sacred author's expression) in the midst of an occasion of sin, and shares his morning meal with the disciples?

As we are approaching the time when we must leave these two weeks of apprenticeship, it is good for us to turn our outlook toward our regular everyday lives. It is there that we will find the presence of the risen Christ. It is a presence in each and every moment of our days. At times, we have a tendency to think that this presence is reserved for our difficult times, for these moments of "Tabor," as they are so numerous at times; in any event, these moments seem to be restricted to times when, in prayer for example, we become conscious of this presence. No, the risen Lord is always there. The Holy Humanity, glorified from this time on, "seated at the right hand of God," is not like us and restricted in his methods of communication by the limitations of time and space. The spiritual stories about apparitions are there "so that we believe," and they teach us of his presence in the dinghy or in the fishing nets, just as he is among the pots and pans or at the impromptu meal at the edge of the lake.

But this happens "through faith." Saint John of the Cross said "it is by night." This world belonging to God into which Christ came was the one of the Transcendent, of the All-Other. Naturally, we are not adapted to it. It is impossible to see him unless he manifests himself. It is impossible for us to feast our eyes on his beauty without dying, so that we can have our turn to enter into the light of his glory.

Consequently, so that we can recognize him, we need signs. We need realities which, acquainted with our blood-and-flesh nature, introduce us, however, to something else. We recognize the flag as a symbol of our national community. And when we see it flying over our national monuments, on public buildings, or at people's homes, we remember that it is a national holiday or that we are commemorating an important date in our country's history.

Jesus left us signs of his presence. But in order to perceive them, we have to know how to recognize them. A stranger that is totally unaware of the habits or history of a country he has come to will not understand all of the significance of the flags flying all over the city. In the same way, in order to perceive the signs of the presence of the risen Christ, we must, as we previously said, "be in his aroma"; we need a heart that listens and is open to admit that God is a God who speaks to us; we must be attentive to the ways he may use for this purpose. God speaks in his own way, but he does so according to his listener. To John, he used the language of a miraculous catch, to Mary Magdalene, the one of the relationship of a master to his disciple, to the pilgrims of Emmaus, he broke bread, and so on. And Thomas, the man to whom "we don't do that," will be invited, because of his "doubtfulness," to touch and to feel.

It is thus, as we have already noted, for each one of us. Signs are given to us which speak to us, according to what we are, what our temperament is and what we have accomplished. Don't be surprised if others don't read them as we do and remain unaffected by them. They have been given to us and are not for others. Spiritual feelings can be very different depending upon the situation. Some of them are very refined, others less so. In front of the empty tomb, it is said of John that "he saw and he believed," yet Peter didn't understand anything and throws himself into the water—one could say that it was his specialty—in order to see; whereas Thomas was particularly difficult to convince. We must have certain "signs of the times" which are adapted to each era, each person, and each concrete collective group.

At all times, if there are signs that address themselves to a particular individual to awaken their faith to be a revelation, there are others through which the totality of believers recognize the presence and action of the Lord. All sacramental equipment belongs in this category. When the priest says: "I baptize you" or "your sins are remitted," he is only a spokesperson, we could say. It is Jesus himself who acts, authentically and assuredly. And even when the priest says, in the name of Christ: "This is my Body," we recognize the Lord as being truly present under the appearance of the bread. We also recognize him in "the breaking of the bread" in a eucharistic sense, no matter what the meaning the exegetes have given to this expression in the specific case of the disciples of Emmaus.

Furthermore, we must not understand this sacramental order in the restrictive sense of the seven signs recognized as such. The Church itself is a sign. When, in the middle of a liturgical assembly, the Word of God is proclaimed, we know to recognize that it is the risen Christ who is speaking. Furthermore, it is the ecclesiastical community as such which delivers us to the presence of Christ, sitting at the right hand of God. Permit us to cite a remark of a catechumen here: "We had a discussion about the relative value of one book of catechism over another. The best book of catechism, to the point of being irreplaceable, is the Christian life on the part of the Church to which children, families, parishes, and others belong. It is there that we enter into contact with the living thoughts of the Lord, the love and the life of the Lord."

All of this brings us back to Teresa, to service to our brothers and sisters, and to obedience.

Lord, you have borrowed the faces of our brothers and sisters for us: may you ask us for a drink, as you did of the Samaritan woman, or may you call upon us, through our superiors, to do what you may. It is certain that even for the Carmelite or the Trappist—and for that matter, the mother of a family!—obedience or service to others leads us more often, and for a longer time, among the pots and pans than it does to prayer. "He is going ahead of you to Galilee; there you will see him" (Mk 16: 7), our Lord said. When you were here on earth, Judea was a country of "pure people"! Galilee, filled with pagans, was a doubtful country: in the eyes of the Pharisees and the scribes, a prophet couldn't have come from there (see Jn 7: 42). It is good for each of us to ask ourselves: "Who are the modern Galileans?"—are they those we find after we pray or after a few days in a retreat? It is to there, Lord, you precede us and await us.

REFLECTION QUESTIONS

Am I at as home with the "least of my brothers and sisters" as I am with the monstrance? If I am not, how can I be more attentive to this oversight or neglect? Do I seek God in all things? Do I recognize that he is present in all things? Do I search out God's face in every person that I meet? God's face is there, looking back at us with love. Can we respond in kind, with love and service? If fear is keeping us from moving into service, can we pray that God might remove this fear? Jesus tells us many times in Scripture, "be not afraid"—are we listening to his comforting words?

DAY FIFTEEN

My Soul Is Serene and at Peace

FOCUS POINT

What does it mean to be "at peace"? Does it mean to be without physical or emotional pain? Content with the status quo? Relaxing, with no work to do? For Teresa, to be "at peace" meant to be with God in the present moment. In fact, many mystics have described it as such. A mind and heart that is set on God, attentive to his voice and faithful to his call, with no lingering feelings for the past and no anxieties concerning the future—this is a person who is at peace. Despite great physical pain and emotional stress, Teresa found the peace to be totally with God, wherever she happened to be.

If I could make your Lordship understand that my soul is serene and at peace, for it is so sure of delighting in God one day, that it seems as if it already has him, yet without his joy. It is as if a person had given a solid investment to someone which she will profit from after a certain delay and from which she will gather the fruit; until a time will come when she will only delight in the assurance of delighting in this investment one day.

(…) She is no longer subjected to the miseries of the world as she previously was. She submits herself to them even more, but they remain exterior to her, as if they concern only her clothing. The soul appears to be the queen of a castle, yet it never loses its peace. At times, this sense of security does not stop her from having a great fear of offending God, and avoiding everything that could stop her from serving him. She is even more attentive to this.

(…) The inner peace, against which consolations and disappointments are virtually powerless, is such that, it seems that this presence, undoubtedly the Three Persons, maintains itself clearly. It is like knowing the experience that Saint John described: that they established their dwelling place in the soul, not only through grace, but so that one could feel this presence, which brings so many benefits with it that one could not possibly describe them (…). This state is almost habitual, except when illness oppresses it. For at times, God wants us to suffer without interior consolation, but never, even by the first move, does the will refuse fulfillment of God within it. This submission has so much force that it doesn't want either life or death, except for the brief instant when it wants to see the face of God. But as soon as the feeling of the presence of these Three Persons is so strong that it appeases the worry that causes this absence, the desire to live remains, if it wishes, to better serve him. And if I could contribute to one soul loving him

more and to better praise him by my intercession, no matter
for how short a time, that seems to be more important than
being in heaven (R6, 1581, Letter to the Bishop of Osma).

———————

These passages are among the last writings that came from
Teresa's pen. They give witness to a sort of celestial peace,
even if some passages show that she was still planted here on
earth.

Teresa spoke a great deal about peace. In her book *Thoughts*
About the Love of God, there is a chapter about false kinds of
peace and another about true peace (P 2 and 3). However,
what we see here is that peace doesn't originate from within
her, Teresa, or from her environment. Things didn't necessarily go as she wanted them to. She suffers from physical ailments.
In the year 1581, if the perspective of a separated province for
the Discalced Carmelite Friars is in the process of becoming a
reality, she doesn't suppress all her tribulations or contradictions. All one has to do is read her *Book of Foundations*. She
tells us herself that the Lord, at times, allows her to suffer
interiorly without consolation. In short, she was far from find-
ing herself in an idyllic condition. But the true peace that the
Lord promised—or the joy that no one can take away (see Jn
16: 22)—doesn't come from being irreproachable. Teresa is
increasingly more conscious of her condition as a sinner. She
knows who she is and she lives in the fear of offending God. It
was a fear, however, that didn't exclude either joy or peace.
For this joy and this peace don't have their origins within Teresa,
but in the knowledge she had of being loved by God. "My
Father and I love each other and we will make our dwelling in
him (her)" (see Jn 14:23).

This joy, then, can be taken away by no one. It is the joy of being loved by God and his indwelling within oneself. "You are precious in my sight…and I love you" (Isa 43:4). It is a joy that expands the heart, as Teresa has already explained, which, by it's very fact, makes one run along the path of the commandments. The majority of the time we think: "Lord, I will seriously get to work, I will roll up my sleeves and then, but only then, will I taste the joy that you promised me." That is a serious error for humans, who are always apt to put ourselves at the center of things and attribute the main role to themselves, even in a life with God! To do that is to put the cart before the horse. The Psalmist re-establishes the correct order: "I run the way of your commandments, for you enlarge my heart [understanding]" (Ps 119: 32).

This peace and joy make people "comfortable with themselves"—just as a motor will run well if it is properly oiled. For those who are the beneficiaries of it, it helps them face life's difficulties with the maximum amount of their psychic strength. In order to get to that point, it is not necessary to have an optimistic temperament or to be what we might call a "force of nature"! God said to Saint Paul: "power is made perfect in weakness" (2 Cor 12:9). Those who have sad or even depressed temperaments could also be witnesses of this peace and joy by giving others the desire to go to the source.

We could say that all of this is just a "sample" of heaven. According to Blessed Elizabeth of the Trinity, heaven could already be experienced here on earth. But, philosophically, there is an important difference between the two cases: eternity is not time! Eternity is a perpetual "now"; conversely, time is an uninterrupted succession of moments, the present being only the indecisive limit between the past and the future.

However, when a soul truly lives united with God, desiring to please him in everything, one of the signs to show that it is progressing on this path consists in the importance it gives to the present moment. The speaker of the present moment and the task of the present moment are the will of God now. We must give everything to it, no half measures; whatever may be the case, if we are clinging to a nostalgic regret from the past that we have abandoned, the desire for something else, or a fear of the future will come along to take its place. If we give everything to it, we adhere with all of our strength to God's eternity, to his perpetual "now." We are completely what he is waiting for, what more could he ask of us? Let us relinquish it all to the judgment of the One who is all goodness! Does the future worry us or devour us through impatience? Tomorrow is tomorrow and next year is next year. The grace of tomorrow will not be given to us today.

There is no more precious grace than the one that "sticks" to the present moment—even if the present requires that we plan for next year! But it is a grace that needs flexibility and availability! For the present leaves a space in each moment for the future with its unexpected surprises. We must then face up to it with flexibility, as a horse obeys his jockey during the race with the least little indications being given it. In other words, we must constantly be ready to be interrupted when obedience or service call to us; to let ourselves be disconcerted by events which take us by surprise which could bring us, in many respects, to burn what we have treasured; to only be unconditional to God alone and not to that which surrounds us. Submissive to the least request from the Holy Spirit, for with him, we will then make up a faultless team.

This submissiveness is not easy. It requires discernment. But it is this submissiveness, when it is habitual, that creates canonized saints like Thérèse of Lisieux and her "little way";

or the group of those who would be candidates for canonization. They perfectly adhere to God. What more could he ask of them? If he comes to get them, they are ready to jump right into his arms!

This is only possible if we have exceptional grace, but it is not forbidden for us to strive for it. And perhaps we will reach it from time to time.

Teresa said: "Consolations and disappoints are virtually powerless against this peace." Saint Paul said the same thing: "If God is for us, who is against us?" (Rom 8:31). We easily understand that Teresa, in the last years of her life, had this celebrated verse come to her which sums it all up:

> May nothing trouble you,
> May nothing frighten you.
> Everything passes, but God never changes.
> Everything comes through patience.
> To those who have God, nothing is lacking.
> God alone is enough.

This verse was found, after her death, in her breviary. Could we have a better ending to the fifteen days we have spent with her than this last prayer?

REFLECTION QUESTIONS

Am I "at peace" with God? Am I able to focus my attention on the sacred present and give myself totally to God at a given moment? Do I pray that God will grace me with the blessing of being present to him in the moment? What types of prayer might benefit me? Might I look into meditation or centering prayer in my efforts to focus more upon God during my prayer?

Bibliography

Bielecki, Tessa. *Teresa of Ávila: Mystical Writings*. Crossroad, 1994.

Bourne, Peter. *Saint Teresa's Castle of the Soul: A Study of the Interior Castle*. Wenzel Press, 1995.

Broughton, Rosemary. *Praying With Teresa of Ávila*. St. Mary's Press, 1995.

Clifford, Paula, tr. *Praying With Saint Teresa of Ávila*. Eerdmans, 1997.

Du Boulay, Shirley. *Teresa of Ávila: Her Story: A Compelling Biography of One of the Most Remarkable Women of All Time*. Servant, 1995.

Hutchinson, Gloria. *A Retreat With Teresa of Ávila: Living by Holy Wit*. St. Anthony Messenger Press, 1999.

Judy, Dwight. *Embracing God: Praying With Teresa of Ávila*. Abingdon, 1996.

Kirvan, John. *Let Nothing Disturb You: A Journey to the Center of the Soul With Saint Teresa of Ávila*. Ave Maria Press, 1996.

Morello, Sam A. *Lectio Divina: And the Practice of Teresian Prayer*. ICS Publications, 1995.

Peers, E. Allison. *The Life of Teresa of Jesus*. Doubleday, 1991.

Teresa of Ávila. *Perfect Love: The Meditations, Prayers, and Writings of Teresa of Ávila*. Doubleday, 1995.